The Road to Dalhousie

THE ROAD TO DALHOUSIE

...

CHARLES SEEMS

PETRA BOOKS
OTTAWA

Library and Archives Canada Cataloguing in Publication

Seems, Charles, author   The road to Dalhousie : memories of the North Shore / by Charles Seems.

ISBN 978-1-927032-09-1 (pbk.)

1. Seems, Charles. 2. Gay men--New Brunswick--Dalhousie Region--Biography. 3. Dalhousie Region (N.B.)--Biography. I. Title.

HQ75.8.S43A3 2013   306.76'62092   C2013-903784-5

© 2013 by Charles Seems. All rights reserved.

Fonts: Papyrus, Garamond 11pt
Petra Books, petrabooks.ca, Ottawa Canada K1S 5P5
Peter Geldart, designer, managing editor.
Danielle Aubrey, consulting editor.
Printed and bound in U.S.A.
9876543210

Any resemblances to persons living or dead or entities past or present are entirely fictional.

You cannot direct the wind,
you can only adjust your sails.

— anon

This book is dedicated to Robert J. Labine
who inspired me to write it
and whose faith in me never faltered.

Special thanks to Mary Routley
for helping me with grammar and syntax.
I also wish to highlight the work of Tracy Seems
who offered feedback on my first draft.

Also by Charles Seems

Ready, Set, Hired! A Practical Guide to Starting a Career with the Canadian Government (General Store Publishing House, Renfrew. 2008)

Préparation, action, embauche! un guide pratique pour amorcer une carrière au sein du gouvernement canadien (General Store Publishing House, Refrew. 2008)

Leadership Gurus Speak Out, co-author. (Experts Who Speak Books, Kanata. 2008)

Drug-Free Arthritis: Secrets to Successful Living (Charo Publishing, Ottawa. 2006)

La Collection Turlututu 16 phonetic readers (Centre franco-ontarien des ressources pédagogiques, Ottawa. 1979)

La Collection Parminou 4 preschool readers (Centre franco-ontarien des ressources pédagogiques, Ottawa. 1988)

Retrouvailles: Couture genealogy (Ven d'est magazine, Québec. 1985)

Selected poetry (Eloizes, Printemps, Moncton. 1982)

Preface

Growing up in a small town is, to say the least ... *interesting*. Everyone knows you – even if you don't know them – so, it's really hard to get away with anything. Someone will always spot you (and tell!), making your own mother seem as though she has second sight. Small towns also cause you to be somewhat "nameless". You are never known by your actual name – well into adulthood. You are always the daughter/son of, the brother/sister of, the niece/nephew of. I even recall being known for several years as "the skinny one who goes around with the tall red-headed one".

Fact is, after a while, you start introducing yourself the same way, just because it makes life easier. Yet, despite the perception of submission, personal identity becomes not only a fight, but a quest.

The other thing about small towns is ... the Fates forbid that you should be different in any way. It doesn't matter if you're gay or straight or something in-between. I well remember being the target of that antagonism and it was not a pleasant experience. As is often said, kids can be cruel and adults rarely intervene because of their own beliefs and prejudices that they spend a lifetime attempting to pass on to their children – thankfully, often without success.

For the vast majority of folks with small town origins, our first step in that quest for identity begins with an overwhelming desire to "get out of town" and seek our fortunes elsewhere. We test our wings, polish our personas and spend a good deal of time learning about the vast differences that exist outside our bubble.

Like the character in <u>The Road to Dalhousie</u>, I was born in the 1950s. Growing up in the '60s was, to my mind, fabulous. When I left my small town to move to the big city, it seemed as though everyone else in the world was working towards new ways of thinking, a revitalized broad-mindedness and an acceptance of differences. So, one would think that in the 21st century, it would be completely unacceptable to make reference to "fags, queers and sissies"! Truth is, on the back roads, in the pool rooms and in the pristine minds of many, those prejudices still fester unchecked.

Big cities have the advantage of being able to absorb huge colonies of people into compact and untouchable little squares. They are faceless and nameless. Nobody cares what someone else is doing unless there is a direct confrontation or a clash of cultures or interests.

Small towns are different and, truth to tell, the Maritimes is a collection of small towns simply spread over a large geographic area. They cling to their traditions – many good, some not so much. Maritime communities can be very supportive; but, they can also be very conservative and exclusive. There are still whispers to be heard of "he's gay, you know" … with that lift of the eyebrow intended to give the impression that this is some sort of amazing revelation.

Recently, a person close to me was diagnosed with progressive Alzheimer's – a disease with horrible consequences that will take his 50-year-old life far too soon. When informed of this, "friends" were heard to say "well, that's not surprising; he is gay, you know". It came as a shock to me to learn that people thought that being gay could cause Alzheimer's!

In the Maritimes, there have been reports of gay couples being refused access to campgrounds and other facilities. In one instance, a

Maritime tourism operator was challenged for his refusal to honour a reservation made by a gay couple – a reservation that he himself had confirmed. When the operator was advised that this type of discrimination could result in cancellation of the requisite operator licence, the operator promptly closed down the facility in protest and has never reopened.

On the positive side, the very first marriage commissioner to be licensed to perform gay/lesbian civil marriages on Prince Edward Island now operates a tourist resort and specializes in gay marriages. Conversely, all of the 40 or so marriage commissioners are legally able to refuse to perform a marriage service for a gay couple based on that marriage commissioner's personal and/or religious beliefs. Given that this is a "civil" marriage ceremony performed *under licence*, the licence should be issued on the premise of "equality for all".

That said, many steps have been taken to enhance acceptance of the gay community in the Maritimes. On Prince Edward Island, for example, "diversity" workshops focusing on the gay community are well advertised and presented through tourism; however, the fact that there is a need to make these presentations also indicates that there continues to be a concern. After all these decades and given the many well-known wise and wonderful gay/lesbian historical figures, and present-day celebrities…such a lack of awareness and acceptance in the 21st century is a very sad comment on our society.

Diana Lariviere

Diana is a PEI Marriage Commissioner and freelance writer. She lives in Prince Edward Island, overlooking the beautiful Northumberland Strait, with her husband of over 25 years and her two dogs. www.weddingspei.ca

iv.

1

The Decision

The noise from the apartment above was unmistakable. I knew they were watching the 1984 Los Angeles Olympic Games. Daniel and his roommate were not close friends of mine; we were civil to each other. It wasn't so much the noise from the television but rather the howls of laughter and the shouts after each successful score that made me want to get into my bed and curl up. The telephone ringing didn't help. Would I answer the call? Easier to simply ignore it. I came to my senses and decided that I would at least find out who was at the other end of the line. After a brief conversation, I went back to where I was sitting.

Summer was quickly coming to an end; the days were getting shorter and the nights cooler. My favourite time of the year was about to begin. Contrary to most people, my New Year starts on September 1st. People come back to the city; students return to campus, cottagers enjoy the last of the season and parliamentarians return from their ridings. Ottawa returns to life; everyone is full of energy—or so it seems.

Queen Victoria had been right in choosing Ottawa to become the capital city of the new Dominion. Had she come herself to see what a spectacular landscape the small hamlet called Bytowne was at the time, she would certainly have been impressed by the waterways, the escarpment and the sheer beauty of its gentle slopes. Founded by Colonel By, Ottawa had grown by leaps and bounds since my arrival in 1976. Most Canadians make the pilgrimage to Ottawa at least once in their lives. For me, that came the year before when I visited a friend who had moved here after graduation.

I remember how I was immediately struck by the number of parks and green spaces everywhere, even in the downtown core, and the mix of gothic, Italianate, rococo and modern architecture that gave the city an air of sophistication. I had discovered an ideal multicultural city. Being able to be immersed in both the English and French culture made it very appealing to me at a time when I was considering where, in all of this vast country of ours, I would settle down. I would need to find suitable employment if I were to survive in this government town. Would I have the skills required? Would I be able to impress a potential employer? At the age of 24, I was not overly confident about my abilities to earn a decent living, but I was naive and bold enough to try.

My first years in the Nation's Capital were not easy; I felt lost in an urban jungle. I struggled to find suitable accommodation and a job that would put food on the table. Slowly, over time, I would acquire the knowledge, the skills and the wherewithal to make it in this most competitive of environments. Making enough money to survive was one thing, but I wanted more than that; I wanted to live in the heart of the city—home of the restaurants, the shops, the art galleries and the universities.

I wanted to live near the shops—where music is made, where art is displayed and where peace and love are more than just words. I knew I had arrived when I moved into an apartment on a street just down from the Parliament Buildings. Richard Steeves had finally made it!

My latest home was a two-bedroom art-deco-inspired apartment at 250 O'Connor Street. I was finally living in the part of town I had always dreamed of. Nothing could remove from me the 'top of the world' feeling I had living in this 1200-square-foot space that had leaded windows, hardwood floors, high ceilings, an art deco fake fireplace and a window in both the kitchen and in the bathroom. It was a corner unit facing east and south with plenty of daylight. The property management team had renovated the whole building and when I came for a viewing, it was the model suite.

Moving to Ottawa from the suburbs, I felt invigorated by the pulse of the city. It had been a mistake to stay away from what gave me a sense of belonging. Although the noise levels were much higher in my new environment, it would only be a matter of time before it became simply background and not the aggravation that afflicted me on that Tuesday night.

Norman's call was unsettling at best. Never persistent or nagging, he had a way of politely asking for what he wanted. That evening, he wondered whether I would join him on a trip to Dalhousie, New Brunswick.

'I'm leaving on Thursday,' said my best friend Norman.

'Not sure I have the time right now' I said.

'Aren't your parents going to Europe in September?' he asked.

'Yes. But I don't see why I should be going home at this time!' I offered lamely.

'Well, this could be the last time you see them alive, you know?' he said, half jokingly.

'Jest if you will, but I have no desire to go back to that forsaken town.'

'Sleep on it, Richard, and call me back tomorrow.'

Groups of young students, already back in the city for the fall semester, were out in the streets celebrating a gold medal for Canada. To this day, I have no idea which event won gold; it wasn't important to me. What was paramount in my mind was the impending decision I had to make: would I regret turning down an offer to visit my aging parents? My mind was out of focus. The sounds from above, the noise from the street below and the excited TV commentator's talk about the Space Shuttle Discovery's maiden voyage clouded my thinking

Retreating to the isolation of my den, I closed the door, pulled down the blinds, plugged my ears and sat half naked on the sofa.

What was Norman really saying to me? Could he see something I couldn't? What if he was a clairvoyant? My mind raced from one thing to another. I had dark images coming to me from recent events such as the Indian Army attacking the Golden Temple in Amritsar in an effort to flush out terrorists, following an order from Indira Gandhi. Would my parents become hostages in some foreign land? This was not an easy decision. Would I regret it for the rest of my life? Mind games, simple mind games! I had no desire to sit in a non-air-conditioned car for the 12 hours it would take to get from Ottawa to Northern New Brunswick.

O'Connor Street was beginning to settle down as the party goers left the neighbourhood bars. Calm was returning to the busy street as it became more subdued throughout the evening.

I felt both excitement and apprehension at the thought of my Mom and Dad leaving for Europe. Mom was not an experienced traveller but she did take us on short trips every year. I was proud of my Dad for having arranged a European bus tour for early September. It would be my mother's first trip outside of North America. And what better way to start her retirement years than taking a first-class excursion to several western European countries!

It was no accident that my father chose September. One might have thought that it was because harvest time was her favourite time. However, my mother had been a teacher for many years and her life revolved around her school, her classroom and her students. At 62, she had decided that it would be nice to live life in the slower lane. My father, having taken his retirement two years earlier, was eager for her to join him so that they could begin to benefit from their golden years.

In my family, the expression *"golden years"* was considered corny, if not downright stupid. How could they be golden when, in fact, most people started to experience serious health problems later on in life? The Golden Age Club was a thriving venture in Dalhousie, a small town where the elderly outnumbered others by 3-to-1. How does one define elderly? Many who went to the Golden Age Club vowed never to go back saying, 'it's all old people who go there'. Growing old was not on my mind but I was painfully aware that my parents were aging gracefully. Time was not to sit still; not for them, not for me.

I felt the world was changing fast; so much was happening around me. Homosexuality had been decriminalised in the state of New South Wales, Australia. And, ironically, almost at the same time, the AIDS virus was identified by a French immunologist. The planet was indeed evolving much faster than I had anticipated. Ottawa was not immune to the spread of AIDS; the first known cases in Canada were being talked about in the press.

With one eye closed and the other struggling to stay focused on the late news, I managed to get the latest on what was happening around the globe. Had I inherited my father's addiction to news stories? I listened to newsreels in English and in French. Curious to know what was happening in all parts of the country, I would tune in to local, regional, provincial and national media before turning to the American news.

Thoughts of Norman's invitation to join him on a quick trip to the 'North Shore' were first on my mind. If I declined, he would have to make the trip on his own. *That alone* was enough to make me want to think seriously about the offer. A childhood friend, he had never let me down. Kind and considerate, Norman had a legion of friends. His humour and his ability to spin a good yarn made him easy to befriend. I enjoyed his company very much and appreciated his concern for me. I would call in the morning and apologise for not being able to accept his gracious offer. Since I would be spending Christmas with my family in Dalhousie, this trip in late August seemed unnecessary.

Sleep came quickly when I finally did get into bed. But it was a hard night.! Every couple of hours, I woke from horrendous nightmares. In one of them, I saw a plane explode over the Atlantic Ocean. There were no survivors! Could this happen to my parents? Norman's words haunted me.

Cars racing on O'Connor Street were the sounds of a new day in Ottawa. Government and high technology workers were going in opposite directions to reach their workplaces. I would wait a bit longer before calling Norman.

'Norman, is that you?' I asked as he answered the telephone.

'No, it's the Queen of England! Who did you expect?'

'Well, your Majesty,' I said 'I've considered your invitation.'

Just as those words were coming out of my mouth, I heard the crash of metal as two cars collided below. My heart dropped as my pressure rose. Accidents at the corner were commonplace but the timing of this one was eerie. I could hear people yelling for an ambulance. In that instant, I reversed my decision.

'At what time are you leaving on Thursday?' I said.

Everything happens for a reason as the saying goes. Although it made sense to me, I wasn't sure of its wisdom in this situation. It was the expression *what goes around, comes around* that got me thinking about how I would want others to remember me in my sunset years. The thought of losing my parents had never worried me before, but now, as I grew older, I often thought of what would happen if my mother was the first to go. My Dad had always been so dependent on her. Would he be able to make a meal for himself if she was no longer around? It was much more comforting not to think of what might happen. My Dad was never the type of person to take care of his health. Chances are he would be the first to go. Visions of mother moaning and weeping did nothing to cheer me up.

Perhaps a trip with Dalhousie's Queen of England would be the perfect antidote.

Most Maritimers who live in our neck of the woods know that if you want to reach New Brunswick in good time, the key is to cross Montreal before the morning traffic. Leaving at 4 a.m., we were on the southern side of the Louis-Hyppolite Lafontaine tunnel that runs beneath the St. Lawrence Seaway long before most Montrealers had their first cup of Java.

Looking directly at me, Norman asked, 'So *Mr. Steeves*, what made you decide to take the trip?'

'The fear that something bad could happen to my parents,' I said, with honesty.

'I didn't mean to frighten you,' replied Norman.

'Maybe your comments jolted me into thinking that my parents will not always be around. They aren't getting any younger,' I said.

In recent years, my mother had mentioned that their bridge partners were all alive and well and that not one couple had lost a spouse. Amongst them, they had wondered who would be the first to go. Was she afraid that her number would be called too soon? Alas, Betty was the first, followed closely by Neil. It became difficult to play bridge. Husband and wife teams that play well and understand each other do not talk across the table—which is a golden rule for serious players of this game. Matching widows and widowers to form new teams did not always work out. When the bridge games were held in our home mother, always the perfect hostess, would make certain that each team was composed of people who had similar ability and approaches to the game.

'Norman, any particular reason you wanted to make the trip at this time of the year?' I said.

'Five days off in a row is good enough for me,' he answered.

'Do you mind if I doze off from time to time? The last few nights have been rough.'

Dozing off, I thought of my parents...

At 5 feet 4 inches, my mother was not particularly tall; she wore size 12 clothing. She had jet black hair, brown eyes and a wonderful smile—when she wasn't frowning. Known for her temper, it was best not to get her going. Meticulous and organized, she liked simplicity in everything. Not one to wear a lot of makeup, she preferred the natural look. She avoided frills and feminine-looking apparel in favour of more streamlined clothing, typically in solid colours. She preferred small patterns, discreet designs and muted tones although she did occasionally like to wear bold colours. In a group of strangers, my mother had no problems introducing herself; she was not shy. Although reserved, she had a good sense of timing and on occasion enjoyed making others laugh and feel relaxed. She would enjoy the camaraderie of her tour group members while in Europe.

My father was the silent type. He stood just a bit taller than my mother. He never worried about being overweight until long after retirement. He preferred having his hair cut short in a brush-cut style. His blue eyes were his most distinguishing feature. Very conservative in dress (which was perhaps influenced by my mother as she chose most of his clothing), he was a proud man. Hardly did he get angry; his eyes did the talking. You could tell when he was upset or when he wanted something but preferred not to ask. He had simple tastes in food and expressed his preferences clearly, hoping that my mother would remember to make things the way he liked them. A creature of habit, he was never fond of change or doing away with something until it was completely worn out.

2

My First Friends

'Hey, Reggie, are you coming out to play?' I said. 'Where to today?'

'Let's try the school yard,' Reggie said.

'When do you have to be back?' I asked.

'You know my Mom! I've got to be home before my father gets back from the Mill. He's working 8 to 4 today,' he said.

Reggie and my cousin Ron were my first friends. Reggie, Ron and I were the three musketeers; for years we were inseparable. Without them, my early years in Dalhousie would have been dull.

Reggie was just a bit younger than me. His parents had built their home in the back yard of his grand parents' house, which was next door to where I lived. As a result, they had no yard around the tiny building. Eldest of a family of four boys, Reggie was precocious. In any game we played together, he had to win, but his fiercely competitive spirit did not get in the way of our friendship.

Strangely enough, I considered him my hero, although, at the time, I don't think I would have used that word. Not as tall as I, he was dark skinned with beautiful brown eyes. He had an intelligent look; he was smart. Reggie kept saying that when he grew up he would become a lawyer. How could anyone so young know exactly what he wanted to be? It baffled me. As with most first born children, much was expected of him; he had to set a good example. His eager parents wanted the best for him and although money was tight, Reggie got most of what he wanted.

Also brilliant was my other buddy Ron, who lived next door to us on the west side. He and Reggie competed to see who could get better grades. Most of the time, they were either 1st or 2nd in their class. In my case, I was lucky to be in the top ten, not that it mattered much to me. As long as my parents were satisfied with my results, I saw no point in trying harder. I had no great plans for the future, nor any idea of the type of job I wanted. One thing I did want for sure was to see the world beyond the borders of our small town. Scenes from faraway places on television and at the movies got my attention; life was different elsewhere.

All three of us played cowboys and Indians regularly. It was Ron who enjoyed this game the most; his world outside Dalhousie seemed to be populated only by actors playing in old-style western movies. But cowboys fell off their horses and got dirty, and that was not my style. Watching men get on and off these huge animals did not stir any passions in me; nonetheless we would imitate Roy Rogers and the legions of others who earned a living making Hollywood movies. We would stake out our territories in our back yards and pretend that we were attacking each other from the saddle of our make-believe horses. For fear of not fitting in, I went along with these games but never really enjoyed them the way Reggie and Ron did. Was I different? I certainly felt different; I tried very hard to conceal my feelings. They probably had figured out that pretending to be cowboys or Indians was not my favourite game. Yet, never once did Reggie or Ron make me feel unwanted; I was always included. The bond that held us together lasted for over five years.

When one of us had a birthday, the other two were invited. Ron's mother always made special birthday cakes with surprises wrapped up in wax paper which we would find when eating a slice of her delicious dessert created for the occasion. We especially liked making a *coke-float* by adding ice cream to a glass of coke; it would fizzle and tickle our noses.

'Hey Reggie, look, I got a dime,' I said.

'Mine is a motel from our Monopoly game,' Ron said.

'You guys are lucky,' Reggie said. 'I didn't find any surprises in my piece of cake.'

I guess Ron's mother could not guarantee that each piece of cake would contain a surprise. At times, the surprise was not getting anything special; it didn't matter to us as we enjoyed being together to celebrate each other's special day. Board games would follow with the usual wicked competitive spirit displayed by Reggie and Ron. Winning was not that important to me; being with good friends meant more than Monopoly money ever could.

Ron, my cousin, the eldest of his family, had two younger brothers. His father worked in the Mill while his mother stayed at home. Not as certain of his future as Reggie, Ron was also considering a career in law but also talked about becoming a doctor or a dentist. Would the game of Monopoly, with its emphasis on getting as rich as possible, impact on the lives of Reggie and Ron?

3

Growing up in Dalhousie

'Did you see that idiot?' Norman said.

'Sorry, I was far away' I replied.

'Where were you?' Norman said.

'Guess I was on the 'North Shore'!' I said.

At the very same moment without warning or looking at each other, we said out loud: There's 'no shore like the North Shore, that's for s-h-o-r-e!'. Together we had a good laugh. Anyone who has ever lived on the 'North Shore' of New Brunswick knows this famous phrase.

Dalhousie, named in honour of Lord Dalhousie, the Canadian Governor General, was laid out in 1826 at the mouth of the Restigouche River which separates the province of New Brunswick from the province of Quebec and which flows into the Baie des Chaleurs. My hometown of Dalhousie was a bilingual community from its very early days. The history of the early setters is not well known.

Jacques Cartier sailed into the Bay in 1534. He landed at Paspébiac Point and was greeted by the Mi'maq. French missionaries started arriving in 1620, visiting regularly. In 1653, the Segnieury of the Restigouche was given out as a land grant to Nicholas Denys who established a trading post at Tjigog (now

Atholville). With the 1713 Treaty of Utretch, the British were ceded New Brunswick and hence Restigouche became English. However, the decisive battle of 1760 for Restigouche brought an end to the French settlement at Point La Garde on the Quebec side of the river. Fifty-five years later British traders came to the Baie des Chaleurs; in 1788, a settler, Peter Bonamy arrived from the Isle of Arran. Inch Arran, with its view of the majestic Bon Ami rocks, on the eastern tip of the city houses the Dalhousie lighthouse and pays homage to Bonamy. Over the years, I have gone back numerous times to admire the beauty of the rocks and the lighthouse set against the backdrop of the Gaspé Coast.

Centred on a pulp and paper mill owned initially by International Paper, the flat land near the waterfront was used to build the largest structure in the settlement. Most of the town is built on the slopes of the Dalhousie Mountain. Getting around can be difficult on some of the steepest streets, and, in winter, driving can be extremely dangerous, sometimes horrendous. I often wondered why the town planners had decided on building a community in such a difficult environment. Perhaps they had not predicted the eventual growth of the town.

Charming as it may have been, there was one major drawback in such a small community: there was no hiding from the neighbours. Everyone knew you and knew what you did. Most people made it their business to know the affairs of other people. Even the local newspaper seemed to feed this un-ending gossip. In June 1958, for instance, the social column contained the following announcement: *On May 28th, Mrs. Edwards of 347*

Montgomery Street hosted a luncheon for the Ladies Auxiliary of St. Barnabas. Thirty women were present. Sandwiches and desserts were served. Mrs. Arseneault, assisted by Mrs. Young, served tea. Father Hillier was also in attendance and blessed the gathering just before he left on a journey to see the Bishop in Bathurst.

The Dalhousie News, a weekly publication, came out on Thursdays. As Mill workers were paid on Wednesdays, it made sense to have the newspaper on the streets when people had money to buy it. At five cents a copy, it was an easy sell. Peddling this newspaper was one of my first paying jobs. My commission was two and half cents per copy sold. 'But there's no such thing as a half penny,' I told them. 'How much will you pay me if I sell 11 newspapers?' I pursued it without getting an answer. Out I went with 50 copies.

I was ambitious and wanted to put some money aside for later projects. Walking down William Street in the direction of the Mill, I would yell, 'Dalhousie News, Dalhousie News, Dalhousie News,' and after a while it sounded as if I were saying, 'da lousy news, da lousy news, da lousy news....' Standing across the street from the Mill in front of a discount store called The Continental, I tried very hard to get the attention of each worker coming out after completing the 8-to-4 shift.

As the paper mill was central in the lives of most of the residents of Dalhousie, Norman and I would always talk about what was happening at the Mill. Were they shutting down the ground wood section for a few weeks or changing some piece of machinery which meant additional work for the on-call staff?

There was always a story to share about this important element of the local economy.

'I hear they are having problems keeping the Mill open,' I said. 'My Dad tells me that a Chinese company is interested in acquiring part of International Paper. I can't imagine what it will be like under foreign ownership. What do the Chinese know about paper-making anyway?'

'What's the alternative?' Norman said. 'If they close the Mill, they might as well close the whole town. It will become a ghost town in no time. There's not much work available other than those well-paying jobs in the ground wood section or in the labs. And think of what would happen to the port facilities, so many huge ships sail into Dalhousie; the chandlers are making a killing.'

Growing up in Dalhousie, I felt pride in belonging to a community that pulled together. The International Paper company cared about its employees. Every year, usually during the Bon Ami summer festival (a pun on the Bonamy Rocks), a parade consisting of most of the social and recreational organizations such as the Lions, the Rotary, the Kinsmen & Kinettes and the Knights of Columbus along with marching bands, majorettes and floats from town and from neighbouring municipalities crawled through the downtown, up Loggie's Hill and down Victoria Street all the way to Inch Arran Park. Miss Dalhousie and her runners-up rode in a convertible or on a float. The mayor would ride in a brightly coloured convertible, if he was lucky enough to find one, or in an expensive car belonging to a wealthy family. Packs of Scouts, Brownies and Guides were also included for good measure. International Paper always had the largest and most interesting float. People living along the route would sit on their front porch to watch the spectacle. At the end of the parade, employees of the Mill would hand out apples and refreshments to the kids.

The festival was held around mid-July. It may have been called the Baie des Chaleurs (meaning 'the bay of heat') but the area was cold most of time. When the winds came from the east over the water, the temperature could drop ten to twenty degrees in a matter of an hour. Having the summer festival at the warmest time of the year was no guarantee that the weather would be fine. By the end of July when the days got shorter and the temperatures cooled, we'd say that summer was over. Made one think about why someone chose the name of *Baie des Chaleurs* for a place that really doesn't get that warm even in summer!

'Would you ever consider moving back to Dalhousie?' I said.

'You're kidding, right?' Norman answered.

4

Dalhousie in the 1950s

There was nothing that would bring us back there permanently. A visit to our respective parents was a must, and we enjoyed going home for two to three days. Any longer and we would go crazy. Yet, the natural beauty of the area, which was lost on us when we were kids, always struck me each time I returned to Dalhousie.

Born in 1952, I grew up in the '50s and '60s. This was a time when television was a new invention. Crowds gathered on Front Street to watch television sets in the display window of Abud's Department Store or at the Lounsbury Furniture Store. Sometimes the curious might have watched a hockey game; most other times the black and white test pattern was all that could be seen. Families who had the means to buy a television set, sold with rabbit ears serving as antenna, would suddenly find neighbours and friends visiting more often than before.

Our main commercial street was the one closest to the waterfront. We called it 'Front Street' although its official name was William Street. Starting at the bottom of the convent hill (officially named Renfrew Street), it went on for four blocks and ended at the bottom of Loggie's Hill, named for a general store that once sat at the Corner of William and George Streets. The paper mill built on the waterfront was at the midpoint on

William Street. Businesses had opened on both sides of the street all along this main thoroughfare.

County government offices, the jail and city hall were built around a green quadrangle which served as a focal point for civic events. A traditional bandstand had been erected to accommodate musicians who performed there on warm summer evenings. Tall oak trees gave this beautiful park an air of sophistication. In later years, the town library would also be erected in south east corner of the park.

With the exception of the planned neighbourhoods that had been developed behind the Hotel Dieu Hospital, most streets in Dalhousie reflected a mix of styles, shapes, and architecture. Built primarily of wood (brick construction being quite rare in those days) houses were typically one or two story structures. Houses were clad in imitation-brick siding or in shingles that, unless painted, would age naturally, turning to a dark shade of grey.

Short growing seasons did not encourage homeowners to put much effort into landscaping. Flowering perennials were most common such as bleeding hearts, daisies and peonies; some avid gardeners planted annuals which may have included begonias, geraniums, and impatiens to liven up otherwise drab front and back yards. Mrs. Hare, who lived up the street from us always had the most colourful yard. As her house was on a corner, her garden was highly visible; newly weds often used it as a background for their pictures.

Each year, by the end of October, cold, strong winds would dominate the weather. The winter season was long and gruelling;

heavy snow would shut down the city many times before the arrival of spring. It was not unusual for the thermometer to drop to minus 40 degrees Fahrenheit; the wind chill factor could reach as low as minus 60 degrees. I remember one of those days when the temperature dipped to that level: I went out for my evening stroll to the Post Office to pick up the mail. Dressed in layers with my face completely covered with the exception of my eyes, I came back home with frostbite on the tip of my nose and small icicles hanging from it.

Even on the coldest of days Mom hung her washing on the clothesline carefully arranging the order of the pieces such that items went in descending order of size. All pants were hung together, all shirts followed a similar pattern, then socks, and the smallest articles were closest to the house and high up enough to be free of the clothes stand. From her perch, she could carry on conversations with Chichi, Reggie's Mom who also had a clothes line; theirs was so much shorter as the space between the two homes built on the same lot severely restricted the length of line.

Nothing beats the smell of clothes dried outdoors! However, there were days when my mother would swear under her breath. I'm sure she said 'the lousy town' as she took in all the clothes from the line and brought them back to the washing machine. Winds from the east brought soot from the Mill which fell on the clean laundry. Westerly winds were predominant but hardly a day went by when they wouldn't quickly turn around and bring us foul odours or soot. The smell of sulphur was unmistakable in that pulp and paper town.

Putting wet sheets out on the clothes line on a very cold day made them hard as plywood. There were few choices for drying bed linens. One particularly cold day, I helped Mom bring in the linen 'plywood' which stood in the kitchen 'till they softened up a bit. Later the sheets were draped on furniture to dry completely.

Snow days meant freedom.

'Reggie, how about building a fort?' I said.

'OK, but it will have to be in your yard,' he said. 'There's not enough space in ours; it could touch my mother's clothes. You know how she gets when that happens.'

'I think the bottom part will open up, like an igloo,' I said.

'Good idea and in there, we'll be warmer,' he said. 'We may need candles as it will be dark.'

Consciously or unconsciously, I tried to get close to Reggie. Patient and respectful, he would never criticize me. I followed his lead. Instinctively, I knew that he would come up with ingenious ways of getting things or organizing a yard game. He was smart and proud of it. He had come first in his class and would probably maintain his standing for years. I, on the other hand, although the son of a school teacher, was not blessed with the same brain power. Failing school was not an option in my family and Mother made sure that didn't happen. When a home-room teacher spoke to my mother about my difficulties, Mother made sure that I got extra tutoring in the evenings.

5

Gas for the Trip

'Are we there yet?' I said with a broad smile on my face.

'Go back to your day-dreaming!' Norman said.

He was a steady driver and never exceeded the speed limit. As far as he was concerned, he didn't have money to spare to pay the stiff fines imposed for speeding. Furthermore, the scenery in rural Quebec was spectacular. We were still far from Quebec City but I was anxious to see the picturesque landscapes east of the city. The highway was less than a kilometre from the St. Lawrence Seaway and, in some places, ran parallel to within metres of the water. Plans were being drawn for a major divided roadway which would be linked to the Trans Canada network of highways. Most often these roads would be in the woods where you couldn't see the bucolic fields. Getting to your destination would be much faster on the Trans Canada, but I preferred the old infrastructure. Despite the ordeal of driving for hours, going through places like Montmagny and St.-Jean-Port-Joli offered great opportunities to see nature at its best. The small sugar loafs at L'Islet, so close to the water's edge that you can distinguish the rough edges of the rock, offered breathtaking vistas. I particularly liked the picnic areas along the road built in strategic areas allowing the travelling public to savour not only their food but scenes reminiscent of art by famous old-world painters.

'Is it too early to eat?' I asked.

'The cooler is in the back seat,' Norman said. 'Help yourself.'

'Egg salad sandwiches, what a surprise!' I said.

'What did you expect, crumpets and tea?' he replied.

'Sorry,' I said. 'No offence. I guess a trip without the egg salad sandwiches would not be the same. Do you realise they give you gas?'

'Speaking of which, I'm down to a quarter of the tank. We'll need to stop soon,' he said.

'Guess farting in it won't help,' I quipped.

'Nor in the car,' he added, 'if you know what's good for you. Do you remember hearing people say, "Estelle Barthe, let a fart, blew the town of Dalhousie apart?"'

'People made so much fun of that poor lady,' I said. 'Yet her musical talents alone outshone many of the town residents. What bothered them most was that she was unconventional. She lived with more than a dozen cats. Rumour had it that she was a lesbian.'

'What part of Lesbos was she from?' Norman asked sarcastically as we burst into hysterical laughter.

'Being different in Dalhousie is tantamount to a death sentence,' I said. 'Just because I liked wearing nice clothes and listening to classical music should not have been a reason for getting odd looks from other people. That is certainly why I left and I'm sure it was the same for you.'

'Couldn't find my prince charming in that smelly town,' he said.

6

My Attraction to Reggie

I attended St. John Bosco School starting in 1958. I was six then. It was there that I began to notice that not all families were the same. Some families were much larger than ours. The ratio of boys to girls was different from one household to another. In my environment, there were a lot more boys than girls. With the exception of my one sister, all the kids in my family as well as those in Reggie's and Ron's families were all boys. I felt comfortable around other boys.

'Reggie, let's go to the basement of your house,' I said.

'What for?' he enquired.

'You'll see when we get there,' I said.

'Hope my mother doesn't catch us,' he said.

'She never comes down here,' I said. 'Anyway, we would hear her and we'd have time to zip up before she opens the door.'

Homes typically had a full foundation and to get to it, there were stairs from inside the house. At their house, Reggie and I could get into the basement through a door that was open to the exterior. This gave us easy entry into a private space that allowed us to engage in activities that would have most certainly been frowned upon by others, especially grown-ups. This is where we compared penis sizes for the first time. There would be many other times, but my recollection of these occasions is very clear, as the danger of being caught was very real, and this intensified the pleasure of doing something that would have meant a lifetime in purgatory, if not hell. But little did we know or care about the consequences. This was curiosity plain and simple and, in our minds, there would be no drastic outcome.

I never really did put a label on my feelings for Reggie. I knew I was attracted to him and I sensed that he was curious about me. I also had the distinct impression that *my* feelings for him were much stronger than *his* for me. But that didn't bother me a bit. I was proud to have him as a friend and I was in awe of his abilities.

In the middle of summer, on a warm evening in July, I convinced my mother that it would be a good idea for me to sleep on the veranda as the ventilation in our second story bedroom was poor; it could be stifling up there and I would be much cooler outdoors. The two sleeping cots that were used for camping would come in handy on this occasion. I also convinced her that it would be safer for me to have Reggie spend the night with me. With both our mother's permission, we were able to spend our first night together. It wasn't fashionable at the time to have sleepovers, particularly for seven-year-old boys, but I guess the concept was not too far from my mind. Would I get to see more of Reggie?

'I hope the two of you will behave tonight,' my mother said.

'Yes mother,' I replied. 'We will be good. You have nothing to worry about us.'

Did mother suspect that I was attracted to Reggie? Did she sense that he was a big influence on me? I was far too young at the time to have had these discussions with her yet I felt some unspoken message from her. She certainly would have frowned upon any physical activity between Reggie and I, but arguably Reggie, was certainly of the intellectual type my Mother approved. We were mere children but I was sure of my attraction for him. I also knew that certain types of people were more acceptable to my mother; being friends with the right kids would be a positive influence.

7

First Signs

Did you hear about Rick?' Norman asked.

'What about him?' I replied.

'Do you know that he's not well?,' Norman said.

'Don't tell me,' I said. 'I hope he doesn't have that dreaded disease.'

'It's called AIDS and anyone can get it. Don't be such a snob about it!'

'Well it's not at all surprising. Rick was sleeping around, wasn't he?'

'It's not for us to pass judgement on the life of others. He is a good person and I admire his sense of caring,' Norman said. 'He is a very loving person; his only goal in life was to be successful and to make others happy. How can that be wrong? He had a tough life at home but made a good living in Ottawa. He worked hard work and was determined. So many have come to Ottawa to seek a better life... Rick made it; moreover, he is the kindest person I've ever met.'

'Sorry, I shouldn't have said that,' I said.

'It scares me that a person could get so sick so fast,' Norman said. 'I read in the newspaper that a person in New York City lasted only two months after he was diagnosed.'

'We still don't know much about AIDS, but in time I hope that we will have a better idea on how to cope with it, how to treat it,' I said.

'Yes, but from what I read, it appears that this is not your ordinary infection that can be cleared up that easily,' Norman said.

'Don't you think that promiscuity is partly to blame?' I said.

'You make it sound like Sodom and Gomorrah,' he said.

Gone were the heady days of the late seventies and early eighties when all was permissible and nobody worried about tomorrow. Now, 1984, it had been two years since we heard about the first reported case of AIDS in Canada—an Air Canada flight attendant who probably had his fair share of fun. Little was known about it and few people wanted to talk about it. In our circle of friends, nobody had shown any symptoms and nobody was really concerned about it.

'Wonder if anyone in Dalhousie has heard about AIDS,' I said.

'That's a good question,' Norman said. 'They may think *It* a big-city problem, but they could be in for a big surprise.'

'Well at least we have excellent doctors in Ottawa should we ever become ill with it,' I said.

'What worries me,' said Norman, 'is how the nursing profession will deal with it. Will the people become like those who have suffered from the plague or from tuberculosis? Will society feel that they should be put away for the sake of the safety of others?'

8

The Airstream Caravan

It was a very hot day in July. 'Wow! Did you see that?' I said to my mother.

She was oblivious to what I had just seen. Two large charcoal-coloured identical cars drove by right in front of our house. I did not have a name for them; I was sure that they were not from Dalhousie. In fact the license plates did not say New Brunswick. They were from the United States but I wasn't quick enough to catch the name of the State. Each car had four doors on both sides of the vehicle making it much longer than an average-size car. It was as if someone had decided to stretch a car to add a few extra rows of seats. This both intrigued and fascinated me. American tourists visiting the Maritime Provinces typically went through Dalhousie during the summer months of June, July and August.

Over the years, these same two elongated cars made their annual pilgrimage to our part of the world. I later found out the name for these vehicles—limousines. Reggie and I had also noticed that the day after the limousines had passed through town, the annual caravan of metallic-coloured motor homes started to stream down Victoria Street. For three to four days, we were entertained by the constant flow of these incredibly elegant trailers being pulled by trucks or powerful cars each bearing license plates from one American State or another.

'I have an idea, Reggie,' I said. 'Let's each get a piece of paper and pencil and write down the names of all the different states.'

'I think we should walk to the corner of Victoria and George across from the FINA gas station and from that point, when they stop, we'll be able to clearly see the plates and write down the names of the states,' Reggie said.

Off we went to spend a few hours. Many of the people in the convoy smiled as they noticed us taking down information from their license plates. Some even waved to us like far-away relatives who were leaving town after visiting for a few days. It was easy to tell that these people were wealthy. The mere size of the vehicles and trailers were a good indication. Not all trailers were identical but they had a few things in common. All of them were made of shiny aluminum and all had rounded corners. We noticed that they had been manufactured by an American company called AirStream. Depending on the time of day at which they were crossing Dalhousie, some of them made a stop at the Inch Arran Park and spent the night. Reggie and I would get there on our bicycles so that we could get a closer look at these astonishing trailers.

Overlooking the Baie des Chaleurs, the tiny peninsula at Inch Arran offers a small beach area with a historic red and white lighthouse to the left. The rolling hills and reddish earth of the Gaspé Peninsula with its crown, Mount St. Joseph, sit directly across the bay. The top of the mountain is used by Catholic pilgrims on the feast of St. Joseph. A tiny chapel had been built so that outdoor Masses could be celebrated on special holy days. Over the years, Mount St. Joseph and the town at its feet, Carleton-sur-Mer, became a popular tourist destination. We weren't sure whether or not the American convoy ever made it over to that part of the region as most Americans spoke English and many Québeçois spoke only French.

Over the years, I would look forward to this annual ritual. I would wonder about all the different places where these people lived. My mind raced from one imaginary location to another, having never been outside Canada. How lucky they were to have the time and money to visit the world in such a privileged fashion! Would I someday be able to travel to far away places?

I was intrigued by the names of the states: Maryland. Was it the land of Mary? Were the people religious? Vermont or 'green mountain'. Were there green hills in that state? New Jersey! Did everyone wear a new sweater? And Delaware. What did Della wear?

The one name that was familiar to us was the state of Maine as it shares a common border with New Brunswick. Every summer, my mother would go shopping in places such as Presqu'ile, Caribou and Bangor. Much of the clothes we wore as kids came from stores like J.C. Penny or Kresgee. I liked the fact that my clothes were different from what could be bought in town at Abud's or Dalfen's department stores. I liked having clothes that were different from what others boys were wearing.

'Reggie, are you interested in going to visit some of these states?' I said.

'Not sure,' he replied. 'I want to go to law school first and then I'll see.'

'What do you want to see?' I enquired.

'Why is it so important for you to go elsewhere?' Reggie said. 'Aren't you happy here in Dalhousie?'

'Not really,' I said. 'There's got to be more to life than this lousy town. Surely, the Good Lord made more interesting places. I want to see as much as I can and go as far as time and money will allow.'

On our way back to the western end of town where we lived, we would take a shortcut through the high part of town near the water reservoir. From that vantage point of about 500 feet above sea level, we would admire the colourful sunsets that changed the whole look of the streetscapes below. The sun setting on the Bay at the P.Q. beach gave off reflections in the water in shades of yellow, red, orange, pink and lavender. The calmer the water, the more stunning the scene was. For brief moments, the town became magical as the evening light reflected on the window panes of the homes close to the water's edge. With dreamy eyes, one could image Ms. Montgomery's house on fire as the effects of the sun gave the illusion that flames were breaking out on the western side of the building.

9

Finding My Place

Did you ever go up the 'shelter' hill all the way to the water tank?' I said.

'Not often,' Norman replied. 'I was always afraid that the reservoir might break open. And if it did, it would really flood the town. Can you image what would happen to the houses built just below it? Makes you wonder why the town fathers allowed it to be built in such a precarious place.'

'When I was a young boy, I would often go to what I used to call *the top of Dalhousie*,' I said. 'It was as if I wanted to see further afield. Not totally satisfied with what was around me, I sought what I did not have; I looked at pictures of places I wanted to visit. It's not that I felt caged, but I felt that there was a whole world out there that I wanted to discover. I knew there were people, out there somewhere, who lived interesting lives.'

'Is that why you left Dalhousie when you were only fourteen?' Norman asked.

'Deep down I knew I was different in ways that were contrary to the norm. I wanted to be able to express myself through art, music and clothing without the fear of having others look at me as if I was from Mars. Growing up in Dalhousie and not fitting in real well with the crowd made me feel like an outsider,' I said. 'I was not a rough kid, never interested in hockey, softball or any group sports. I found pleasure in the arts; I loved music and, for a while, I even painted. One does get branded as a sissy in a tough-boy town if you don't participate in sports or chase the girls. I'm sure I've already told you that a relative of mine called me a sissy. I wasn't sure that the word was appropriate but I knew what she meant and it hurt.'

'I know what you mean,' he said. 'We were all boys in my family and my mother had wanted at least one girl. As I was the least strong kid, my Mom made me wash dishes, clean floors and make beds. I resented that but what could I do? I needed pocket money so doing household chores was an easy way to get what I wanted. It paid for my cigarettes.'

'Do you hold a grudge against her?' I asked.

'In my teen years, I kept my anger to myself,' he said. 'I had very few ways of venting ... talking back was never an option. I had a strong bond with my mother even though I felt abused in some ways. What was it like for you?'

'It was very different from your experience and yet I sense similarities,' I said. 'My Mom suffered greatly because of her arthritis; the look of pain on her face made me want to do as much as I could to make her life easier. For example, while she was out having her hair done, I would dust the furniture, vacuum the floors and tidy up. When she came back from the hair salon, she felt great and with the house looking as it did, her smile was worth millions to me. Was I looking for approval? Perhaps. It was my way of thanking her for all she did for us kids.'

I was the fourth child in a family of six. We were all boys with the exception of my sister Claire. She was the second eldest and my mother's pride and joy. With any large family, you tend to gravitate to those with whom you have affinities. In my case, my closest ally was Claire. She was always wise and ready to help me when she could. During mother's difficult times, she became a surrogate mother to all of us.

With the exception of Ernie who suffered from cerebral palsy, my other brothers were achievers. They were into sports, girls and having a good time. I felt very different from them; in my teen years, I felt that I was way too different to be part of my family. I felt isolated because I was different. But I knew that no matter what I did, I could not change the very person I was. I would always prefer figure skating to hockey. Having the darkest complexion of any of my siblings, I was the target of name-calling which was hurtful. One of my brothers called me 'tar pot' and when I got angry at him for teasing me, he would then call me 'snowflake' which made matters worse. In return, I called him 'elephant' as he was the biggest person in the family.

Nicknames were common; almost everyone I knew had one. Sometimes it was a shorter version of a name such as 'Beth' for 'Elizabeth'. In some instances, the nickname was derived from something the person did or liked. 'Onion' was the nickname of my friend Michael because he ate raw onions and reeked of them. Initials were used as names as well; Pierre André Blanchard was known simply as PA. Doubling of a syllable was also popular. A girl named 'Louise' would likely be called Loulou. For years, people's real names were unknown to me such that, in some cases, I was convinced that their nicknames were their actual names.

We were a middle class family living in a very modest house on a busy street. As practicing Catholics, we were fortunate to be living less than one block away from our parish church, St. John Bosco. Attendance at Sunday mass and high holy days was mandatory with ex-communication as potential punishment for not following church commandments. During Lent and Advent, we were highly encouraged to attend more frequently, which we did. The church building itself was rather basic. In fact, there were several almost identical churches in the same diocese all with large double doors and single east and west doors on the front of the building. There were side doors located on either side of the sanctuary which were most useful when vacating the building. The high vaulted ceiling and walls were tar sheets (commonly called 'tentest') which had been painted in shades of beige, light brown and a soft yellow, alternating the colours to highlight the architectural features. There was no comparison with the much finer St. John the Baptist Church in the eastern part of town, built in the gothic style complete with large and impressive artwork; the main fresco over the altar depicted St. John baptizing several people in a creek. Obviously, we were the poor parish and could not afford elaborate and detailed art work. It made me feel inferior to those lucky enough to belong to that congregation.

Just behind our church was the St. John Bosco School which was operated by the nuns of the Daughters of Jesus congregation. They had settled in most towns and villages in the northern part of New Brunswick. The sisters offered instruction up to Grade 7 after which students went to High School. As there weren't enough nuns for all the classes, lay people were hired to fill the vacancies. The quality of education was quite high as the nuns were well trained and spent their entire days devoted to teaching and a daily ritual, praying.

Education in my family was the prime focus of our being. My mother had also been well educated. As the oldest daughter in her family, she had been allowed to go to 'Normal' school in Fredericton where she took teacher training. She became an elementary school teacher in rural areas around Dalhousie before she married. In raising a family, she ensured that each of us would benefit from the best education possible. My parents wanted us to have a university education, and to help prepare for a higher level schooling they were ready to consider good boarding schools. Expensive as they were, but not so dear that we would be denied the option of going to one of them if we so chose, both my brother Phil and my sister Claire studied in boarding schools run by religious orders in places such as Jacquet River, St. Louis de Kent, Tracadie and St. Basile to name a few.

I thought long and hard about going away to a boarding school as my older siblings had done before me. Could it be a way to get out of this place and learn about the world out there? At a Sunday mass, Father Mallette had informed the congergation that a new boarding school was opening in the city of Bathurst, just 50 miles from Dalhousie. The all-boys school was open to students in Grades 10, 11 and 12 as well as those wanting to continue their education at the Collège de Bathurst. Built with money from all over the diocese, the new Petit Séminaire St. Charles Borromée had just been completed; secular priests (those not assigned to a parish) from the diocese would be selected to become instructors at the school. From the pictures I had seen, the campus consisted of four buildings: the chapel, the main building (housing the classroom and library at one end and the dormitories at the other end with administrative offices in between), the sports and entertainment building and the dining hall. What was remarkable were the fieldstones that had been used to build the walls.

I showed an interest in going to the Petit Séminaire so the parish priest was invited to our home to discuss the possibilities. To be admitted, one had to be recommended by the parish priest.

The decision was made. I would finish Grade 9 at Notre Dame High School in Dalhousie before continuing my studies in Bathurst.

'Getting back to your question about wanting to leave Dalhousie,' I continued to Norman, 'the two years I spent at the boarding school in Bathurst were perhaps the best years of my life in New Brunswick. Thinking back on all the advantages boarding school offered over regular school, I can't help but wonder if I would be the same person today had I not gone there. We were exposed to classical music, fine arts, performing arts, photography, and geography, history and languages and so many other interesting subjects. The knowledge and experience of our teachers was overwhelming. They had a wonderful way of getting us interested in every possible subject. How fortunate I was to be able to be there to absorb as much as I did. It's sad to think that today's kids will not have the kind of opportunity I had.'

'Yes, you were lucky to have parents that placed so much importance on education,' Norman said. 'For me, the world opened up when I moved to Ottawa. I furthered myself by learning all I could from smart people I met since I arrived in the big city. Mine was not a formal education but rather self taught; I got help from so many good friends. I'm glad you didn't forsake me because of my lack of schooling!'

'Good friends are hard to come by; it would have been silly of me to dismiss you simply because you didn't have the same opportunities or background as I had,' I said. 'Honesty and sincerity are far more important hallmarks that I look for in the people I meet. Money, education, status and titles don't necessary point to the best people. I have come across a lot of different types over the years but few with the qualities I value. I don't judge people on the thickness of their wallets, nor on the number of diplomas on their walls, or who they know in high places. I am more apt to be blown over by a person who is happy and passionate about something or other. When I met you, Norman, I knew that I had found a friend for life.'

10

Father Mallette's Sermon

Mom and Dad had gone to early mass at 9 a.m. As I didn't get up early enough to join them, my only choice was to attend the longer 11 a.m. high mass. The choir sang beautifully at high mass, which made it palatable for me. I sat alone in the 5th or 6th pew. As more people came in, I had to move further down the pew losing my preferred aisle seat. It was just as well as I didn't have a large amount of money to put into the collection plate.

Father Mallette, a good French Canadian priest, was saying mass that morning. He was known to be feisty and could be rather arrogant at times. Altar boys lived in fear of him particularly when he was in the confessional booth and there was no other priest available.

It was in early May; the windows of the St. John Bosco church had to be opened to let in fresh air. That was unusual as warm weather did not normally come until the end of June. My attendance at the 11 a.m. mass without my family was also unusual. Being a bilingual parish, masses alternated between French and English and this morning's high mass was being celebrated in English. Father Mallette's English skills were excellent but his pronunciation was off a tad on some words.

Father was well known for his long sermons. At the age of seven, they appeared like an eternity. I tried hard to remember some of the things he said because I would be questioned by my mother once I got back home; my attention span was short and I would eventually spend more time looking at the colour scheme and the architectural elements of the building rather than paying close attention to the morals being taught. I was brought back to attention when I heard Father Mallette say rather loudly and boldly 'shell fish.' I knew as Catholics we were expected not to eat meat on Fridays and therefore most people ate fish. But I couldn't understand why he was talking about shell fish. Lobsters were abundant in the Baie de Chaleurs and maybe he was making the point that we should buy from our local fishermen. But as I tried to follow what was being said, I realized that he was saying 'sell fish.' Now why on earth would he be talking about selling fish during his sermon? On listening even more closely, I understood him to say that he thought many parishioners were selfish and not concerned about the good of the community as a whole. This would be a story that I would not share, even with my Mother.

After the final blessing and after the priest had left the sanctuary, the faithful hurried out of the pews to the nearest exit, some using the side doors to get out as quickly as possible. I joined the queue walking to the main doors. People were pressed against each other and obviously anxious to get out of the building. As we got closer to the doors, just past the last pew, I was pushed to the point of almost being knocked into the confessional booth. I recovered just in time and quickly left through the west door. I ran down the stairs and got home in less than five minutes. When I walked in with face flushed, I looked at my mother and I remember saying, 'I nearly fell into the shack.' My mother laughed heartily and asked for further details. When I explained what had occurred, she understood what I meant by 'the shack.' Since then, I have called the confessional booth, 'the shack'.

11

Why I left Dalhousie

Here we are in 1984 in what should have been, according to George Orwell, a *Big Brother* society,' I said. 'Orwell may not have been entirely wrong; he may simply have had the year incorrect. As we move into an era of automation, it will become increasingly easy for governments and large companies to know all about us. I hate to think that an organisation or government would want to play God. What if everything we did was caught on camera? Would we need to have access codes or would our bodies become our sole identification? I'm not sure I would want others to know my private thoughts. There have been times when I think I could have been ostracised for my beliefs. *That* book would make a good movie, don't you think?'

'I haven't read it,' said Norman, 'but it doesn't seem the kind of book that would interest me. Have you seen the movie 'Terms of Endearment' with Sally Fields?'

'Yes I saw the movie but the main actress was Shirley McLain,' I said. 'The message of the movie is quite simple and powerful: different people show their love in different ways. I wonder how far we can go on that theme. *Big Brother* would probably not be in agreement with my version of life and love.' The movie's message is that love, regardless of the type, is always a good thing. For gays, this powerful message countered the message repeated by hate groups that love between men was not right, was not appropriate and was sick, plain and simple. It was often through movies that gay men picked up positive messages that helped them go on. This was one movie that helped me immensely.

'In many ways, that's the real reason I left Dalhousie,' Norman said. 'I could not be the real me. I could not express my love in forms that would have been acceptable in small town

New Brunswick. Times may have changed but on every trip back to that lousy town, the same feelings of awkwardness come over me. But since my mother moved to Ottawa a few years ago, her views of the world have changed; she accepts people as they are. I'm so fortunate to have her close to me.'

Our mothers grew up in the same town but were miles apart in their ways of thinking and doing. We were brought up very differently. My mother was not as tolerant of differences as was Norman's mother. Strong willed ladies they were and oddly enough related through marriage: my mother's brother had married Norman's aunt on his father's side.

'Should we stop in La Pocatière for lunch?' Norman asked.

'It will be early afternoon by the time we get there, but we should stop anyway,' I said. I hadn't told my parents that I was coming for a visit. 'We'll meet half of Dalhousie at L'oiseau Bleu. Most of them will be on their way to Montreal to see a baseball game or to go shopping. It never fails, every time I've been to that restaurant, I always see people I know. We are such creatures of habit.'

'I can take over after lunch and drive as far as Rivière-du-Loup,' I said.

'The break would be nice,' said Norman. 'My legs and feet are getting numb.'

12

Disengaging with Reggie

'Reggie, did you light the candles on the main altar?' I said.

'Oops, I forgot about them,' he said.

'Can you imagine the look we would get from Father Mallette if mass started and he saw that the candles were not lit?' I said. 'Just last week, when Bobbie Cool was serving mass, he was pouring the wine into the chalice rather slowly when Father stuck his thumb in the cruet, held it upside down and just about emptied it. At least he didn't yell at him as he has been known to do.'

'Did you know that there is a jamboree concert in the church basement on Sunday night?' I said. 'If you want to get in free, you'll have to attend the 8 p.m. vespers. We usually hang around and after Father Mallette has finished removing his vestments, he normally takes us down using the back stairwell. He makes sure that we get in without paying. That is about the only benefit of being an altar boy.'

'Not sure my mother will approve of me getting home late when I have to get up the next morning to go to school but I'll see what she says,' Reggie replied.

I wasn't sure if he was trying to find a way out of the situation. At times, I thought that he preferred not going to the church shows as he was so keen on school, nothing should detract from it. As the years went by, Reggie and I would see less of each other. In 1962, his father had accumulated enough money to buy a new house in the up-and-coming Dastous subdivision behind St. John the Baptist Church. Now belonging to a different parish, we went to different schools and we no longer saw each other in church. A bicycle ride to his new home took about 15 minutes; after a few visits, I got the impression that he wanted to move on and be with his newfound friends. For a couple of years afterwards, I felt lost without his companionship.

Summertime was a hard time to be without good friends. My only hope was to get a glimpse of Reggie with his family at the beach. Just outside the town limits and before the village of Charlo, is the Eel River Bar. On one side of the road is the Baie de Chaleurs and on the other, the Eel River, which has one of the longest natural sandbars in the world. At one end, water is fresh and at the other, water is salty. On warm days in July and August, cars would be lined on either side of the road; bathers to the north and clam diggers to the south. Whole families would come and spend the day. Sundays were particularly busy. With any luck, I might run into Reggie.

Near a bridge linking the Eel River Bar to the First Nation's community, vendors in brightly coloured trailers sold habitual snacks such as hamburgers, hotdogs, fries, chocolate bars, and cotton candy. I can remember making my way, barefoot and in swimming trunks, to one of the kiosks to get a bottle of Fanta Orange. The aroma of the sea water combined with the smell of camp fires on the beach was unmistakable. All of this contributed to a carnival-like atmosphere which was intoxicating. As the day wore on, the crowds got thinner. Many stayed for clambakes and bonfires. Guitars, stored in the trunks of cars, were retrieved and no sooner were they tuned that our voices would join in to make the most memorable music.

Although I didn't see Reggie very often at the beach, just the possibility of connecting with him was enough to make me want to spend time at the Eel River Bar.

13

Heroes and Mentors

'It's been a long while since I've driven your car,' I said.

'I like it when my subjects do the driving for me,' Norman said.

'Well enjoy it while you can, your Majesty,' I said. 'I really don't like being behind the wheel but I much prefer highway driving to city.'

'Would you prefer being on a bicycle?' Norman asked.

'It's been years since I've enjoyed riding a bicycle,' I said. 'When I was young, I would spend hours going from one part of Dalhousie to the next. To avoid the hills, I would go horizontally as far as I could; then I would find a gentle slope that would allow me to get to higher ground without the effort that would have been required had I gone straight up. I would cycle from William to Queen Street towards the west end and then up Bearse Street, a short slant that led to Victoria Street. Once on Victoria, I would make my way to the east end and make a right turn on Bujold and another right on Grey. By continuing on this street, I could get to the top of the Convent hill (Goderich) without much effort. Using this route, I would ride by Reggie's house.'

'Who is Reggie?' Norman asked.

'You know that young lawyer on Adelaide Street,' I said. 'He was my hero when I was a young boy. Later, though, I had another one. Morton was my team captain in Cubs. He was tall, polite, engaging—all together great guy. What impressed me the most was that he treated all of us the same way regardless of our levels of ability. I was rather shy and not at all sports-minded then, but he was still able to get me to join team games during our weekly cub meets. I never forgot him; I followed his progress until I heard he joined the Royal Canadian Mounted Police. Did you have anybody to look up to?'

There was no answer to my question. It may have been rhetorical but I can't remember my intent. Norman's early years had been difficult. Not having many friends, he stayed close to home obeying the commands of a demanding mother and a mostly absent father. He seldom spoke of those difficult years even in the privacy of our respective apartments. When things got rough or annoying, he used humour for self-protection, which effectively calmed things down. Formal education had been his cross to bear, while learning did not come easily to him. When it came to street sense, he had it in spades.

Our friendship started in my last year of high school. We would probably have met earlier had it not been for the two years I spent in the boarding school in Bathurst. The details of how we became friends are lost to me, but soon we were inseparable companions; it was as if we had always known each other. Like me, he favoured music over sports, kindness over bullying, love over war and cleanliness over filth. Never a slouch, Norman worked while attending high school. Being a waiter in a restaurant can be daunting at the best of times, but Norman was a real professional. He had a remarkable way with clients; everyone forgave the outrageous things he said to the people he served in order to get them in a good mood. They would even overlook his clumsy grammar.

14

First Cruise

Great, I thought to myself, it's Sunday and with any luck Mom and Dad will take us out for a 'drive'. Our Sunday afternoon outings had started shortly after my father had bought his first car. Not that we went very far, but escaping the town was a welcome relief for me. Often, we would drive westward to

Campbellton to visit relatives. Aunt Annie and her husband Cameron lived with their son, Mike, in a small house on Dufferin Street. While the grown-ups were busy talking about adult matters, Mike and I would wander around the city. For two 12 year old lads, our conversations were pretty mundane and usually centered on family matters or school issues but were never about girls. Unlike Dalhousie, Campbellton was much more sophisticated, with a larger population. Further up the Restigouche River, Campbellton is much flatter than Dalhousie. A short ferry across the river and you were in the province of Quebec (in the village of Pointe à la croix).

Mike insisted that we take the ferry across the Restigouche. He and his parents had discovered the restaurant 'Marie Antoinnette' which was attached to an Esso garage right next to a motel overlooking the Restigouche River. It had become one of their favourite places to go for a light meal or snack.

We boarded the 2:20 ferry to Cross Point just minutes after we heard the all-aboard whistle. My mind raced as I knew that my parents would probably not approve of this. What if we couldn't get back in time? Mike had done the crossing a number of times and assured me that we would be back on Dufferin Street by 4 p.m.; nobody would be any more the wiser.

We stood for the whole crossing which took about 15 minutes. That way we could see the city of Campbellton diminish in size the further away we were from the dock. In no time, we looked in the opposite direction to the wharf where the vessel would be docking. During the crossing, I felt free as the air; the feeling of going to a new destination made me happy. Was this the feeling that those Americans travelling in caravans had when they came to the Maritime Provinces? If it was, then I could understand how enjoyable it was to travel to distant places. Cross Point was not an exotic location but it could have been Bora Bora for all I cared. The excitement grew as the Ferry got closer to the dock. Mike started telling me more about the restaurant, what to expect.

It was only steps away from the dock; in a matter of minutes we were at the door of the Marie Antoinette. Even in the middle of the afternoon, the place was busy and getting a booth close to the windows wasn't a sure bet. Perhaps the stools at the counter would be just as good I thought. Just then, two young girls sitting at a booth got up and left. We both made a mad dash to get the booth before someone else did. The waitress was none too happy as she had yet to clear the table; however, we think she understood why we preferred the window seats.

It wasn't that the place was spectacular, but for two young boys this was the height of elegance. On my cousin's recommendation, we ordered the traditional 'banana split sundae' with butterscotch, crushed walnuts and a cherry topping. The portion was huge so we decided to share it. Thank God Mike had the foresight to think about the money to pay for this treat. Having seldom been in a restaurant, and the few times I had been with my parents, I had not thought about the cost of what we were ordering. Mike, on the other hand, was far more street-wise than I was. His weekly allowance was ample to cover the bill. With bellies full and smiles on our faces, we made our way back to the pier for the return trip of my very first cruise. In the years that followed, we did many such trips before the Van Horne Bridge was built connecting the Gaspé Peninsula with Northern New Brunswick.

We arrived back at Dufferin Street just in time. My parents were saying their good-byes on the front porch. My mother looked at me with inquisitive eyes as though she guessed that Mike and I had been up to something she would not have approved. In polite company, she remained silent.

'I've made some cookies,' Aunt Annie said. 'Would you like to taste them?'

'How can I refuse? You make the best and biggest cookies,' I said.

Under the scornful look of my mother, Mike and I were ushered into the tiny kitchen where a plate of large butterscotch chip cookies and two glasses of milk were waiting for us. It would have been impolite to say that we had already eaten; we weren't about to admit to having left the province without permission. I gobbled down two cookies, emptied the glass of milk and thanked Aunt Annie. I rushed out the door and into the car where my parents were waiting patiently.

I felt a strong bond between my cousin Mike and myself. It wasn't just the fact that we were related, but also that we were very close in age and shared common interests. As with most boys our age, at twelve we had little interest in girls. Aunt Annie was my mother's younger sister; she seemed more liberated than my mother, being very open and outgoing. She worked in a government office earning a good salary and enjoyed the perks that came with a comfortable income. Uncle Cameron also worked in the same office, and he too had a good job.

Together they were able to buy the finest of cars, which impressed us. How I remember when they bought a dark green Chrysler New Yorker—built like a tank. Aunt Annie was so proud of that vehicle; it was a mark of achievement, a status symbol. She boasted that her salary was in the five-figure bracket, making even more than her husband.

One Saturday afternoon, they were visiting my grandparents who lived next door to us in Dalhousie; Aunt Annie asked Mike to wash the car which he did on numerous occasions. Usually, if I was around, I would help Mike, but I had been away at a summer camp and had just arrived home when I noticed the Chrysler New Yorker parked in the yard next door. I went out to offer my help but Mike was almost finished. I remember vividly the look of horror on Aunt Annie's face when she came out of the house and saw how the car's paint job looked lacklustre. She went into a rant about Mike washing her car with Javex. The jury is still out on what Mike used to wash that vehicle. That was the last time he was allowed the privilege of cleaning the family car. He was never asked again nor did we dare volunteer.

15

Showing Love

According to the signs, we were approximately 50 miles west of Rimouski where the road turns inland and away from the seashore. Villages were further away from each other with densely wooded stretches in between. I had been driving in silence for an hour when Norman came back to life.

'Had a nice snooze?' I said.

'I'm not sure if it's the lack of scenery or your reminiscing about Dalhousie that made me sleepy,' Norman said, 'but I now feel refreshed. Let me take over driving.'

'Did I ever tell you that Aunt Allie taught me in Grade Two?' I said. 'Well she's your aunt too. Have you ever been her student?' I said. 'She and my mother were good friends. As teachers, they had things in common other than the fact that her husband was my mother's brother, the eldest of the siblings in her family. I can see some family resemblances between you and Aunt Allie. She also used humour in a very special way. I wonder if my Mom was influenced by her. What do you think?'

'Your mother's wit is quite special,' Norman said. 'I can't get over the number of expressions she uses. I like *my name is Sandy not Sandy Claus!* Does she have one for every situation?'

'Probably, I have over 100 expressions written down in my notebook,' I said. 'A few weeks ago, I started writing them down as they came to me. Last time I was in Dalhousie, Mom used a number of them knowing only too well that I get the greatest kick out of them. Some come from her siblings, others come from radio and television commercials and some she just makes up as needed depending on the situation. To a certain extent, she uses humour in a similar way as you do. When things go wrong or someone needs to be told something unpleasant, she finds an expression or she creates one that will deliver the message she wants to convey in a funny, truthful manner. Some are crude, some are silly, but they are all characteristic of her.'

'When I hear you talk about your mother, I sense the incredible love you have for her,' Norman said. 'I know you have had hard times with your Mom. She was a tough parent but in the end, I think she did what she needed to do. As kids, we weren't angels; we needed to be told what was appropriate and what was not. As a school teacher, your mother had an image she wanted to protect or should I say a reputation to uphold. Yet, despite any differences you may have had with her, you both got along so well. Are you able to tell your mother that you love her?'

'We were never very demonstrative in my family,' I said. 'Showing one's love was seldom overt. Was I afraid that such emotions were better left in check? My father's love was oblivious to me for years. I think he expected more from me than what I was capable of at the time. I didn't even know how to stand around him. I felt that he often thought I was a useless individual not knowing how to mow a lawn, use a hammer or tie ropes. He had precious little patience to teach us kids.

As a stevedore foreman at the Dalhousie dock, each person reporting to my Dad had specific tasks to perform and each was supposed to know the parameters of his job. His standards were high; he was unwilling or unable to accept less than excellent performance. Loyalty to the company and perfect attendance was expected. Did he expect the same from his children?

My mother was aware that I felt distant from my father. One night, at about 8 p.m. when typically I would go out for the evening, I wanted to ask my father about borrowing the car. As he was asleep on the living room sofa, I wasn't about to wake him and ask him for the keys. Mother, sensing what was happening, said, 'Look, he took his cars keys out of his pocket and left them on the coffee table before lying down. He knew you would want to use the family car tonight.'

The keys had been carefully placed so that I would see them walking into the room. He hadn't asked if I wanted to use the car; he simply made it available to me in his own way. This simple gesture brought tears to my eyes; it was one of the first times that I realised he cared for me. Had I missed many more of these signs in earlier years? Probably, I wasn't looking; I was too busy worrying about my own personal business.

'I don't think we tell our parents often enough how much they mean to us,' Norman said. 'My parents are younger than yours but I still feel that they are aging fast. Now they have separated, I don't see my father as often; to some degree that might be for the better as I was never very close to him. Yet I am his flesh and blood and when he's around me, he's as a proud as a peacock. I'm not a jock like the others in my family yet he stills accepts me for the person I am. My mother, on the other hand, acknowledges that she demanded too much of me when I was living at home. I don't begrudge her those years when maintaining the family home became such a chore; she needed help and I was the obvious one to give her that support. One does what one has to in order to survive. She was in an unhappy marriage but would not abandon her children for the sake of freedom; she stayed, but spent a lot of time away from the house when my father was around. So, as you can see, it wasn't easy for me either.'

We both mulled over our familial relationships knowing that whatever pain we had experienced in childhood was more than compensated for in our lives as adults in a world that was opening up to diversity and acceptance. As I closed my eyes Norman saw that I needed some time to think. I made a pledge to myself to ensure that my parents would know of my love for them during the upcoming weekend in Dalhousie.

16

Brown-Eyed Girl, Blue-Eyed Boy

On my first day in this boys boarding school, I was immediately approached by Barry who wanted me to be his special friend. It sounded as if he wanted me exclusively to himself.

'Barry, I want to be friends with all of the boys here in this school,' I said.

'Well I think you're special and I would like you to come to me when you have problems,' Barry said. 'I know the ropes in this place; you will need some protection.'

Was this like a prison environment where you need an older, more experienced protector to guard you against the evils that might be inflicted by others? Little did I know that in any boarding school, it pays to know the right people!

Barry was a year older than me and knew from experience that older guys would prey on the younger new recruits. There was also the possibility that some evil bully might molest me. A native of Bathurst, his family lived within a few miles of the school. Judging from the marks on his face, it was easy to tell that he had had a lot of acne in earlier years. Facial hairs had started to sprout; this required that he shave every couple of days which made him proud. I guess he thought it was a rather manly thing to do. 'Old Spice' was his cologne; just the smell of it was enough to make me puke. The fact that my father used the same product didn't help; to me, it was an old man's fragrance, one that was a real turn-off. Not one for strong scents, this alone was enough to have me running in the opposite direction every time we met in the hallways. He eventually got the message.

Another guy, by the name of Larry, was also lurking in the background. Even older than Barry, Larry was also very keen on being my best buddy. He warned me of others with bad reputations because of past deeds never forgotten in such a closed community. Larry was kind and considerate. An avid card player, he encouraged me to learn how to play 'tens' which is quite similar to bridge but does not make use of the 2s, 3s and 4s, regardless of suit. The bidding is based on 100 points. Like bridge, you bid based on the strength of your cards and what you think your partner may have in his hands. The bid can be raised by your partner to indicate support. Aces were worth 15 points, face cards 10 points, 10s and 5s were worth their face value. Bids were based on a suit or no trump as called by the bidders. I quickly caught on and soon realised that there was quite a rivalry between clans of boys in the school. Had I aligned myself with the right gang? Time would tell. Cheating was part of the game; pointing to one's heart meant a strong suit of hearts. Tapping on a finger meant lots of diamonds while a slight pick of the nose indicated strong spades in hand. To signal a strong support in clubs, tapping all four fingers on the table sent the right message.

For those of us who weren't sports-minded, playing cards and listening to music in the student lounge was a favourite activity. At the centre of the room was a huge fieldstone fireplace which was lit most weekend nights during the winter months. The lights were dimmed once the card games were over. From a stack of records supplied by the priests, someone would put on soft music to go with the mood created by the crackling of the fire. At times, sitting in a semi-circle in front of the fireplace, we had heated discussions about current events or issues dealing with the school. Other nights, when we were tired, everyone sat around silently and enjoyed the peace and tranquility of the moment. I savoured these exquisite moments; they were unforgettable.

There were few opportunities to escape the confines of the school other than by attending a concert at the Auditorium of the Collège de Bathurst. There I saw a very young Nana Mouskouri long before she was well known around the world. That was a delightful event. On Saturday afternoons, we were allowed to venture into town. It was a rather long walk to get there but nobody was about to complain. In groups of three or four, we would make our way into the downtown core of the city. My favourite department store was *Kent's*; my friends would follow me in and we would check out the men's wear department. What made the experience unique was paying for the goods you wanted to purchase. A salesclerk would write up a slip listing your purchases; you handed over the money which was put in a large glass and metal bullet along with the bill of sales. A vacuum system sent the bullet all the way to the accounting department on the third floor for verification before returning it to the originator for completion of the transaction and remittance of the change to the customer.

Before heading back, we always made a stop at the Bathurst Grill on Main Street. We would find an empty booth and crowd into it. Each booth had its private listings of hits that could be played from the main jukebox. By inserting a quarter in the machine, you could play three selections. You did not always hear your selections in a row, as requests from other tables would be taken into the queue and played sequentially. My favourite song was 'Brown-Eyed Girl' by Van Morrison; it got chosen at least once on each visit. Once the music had been selected, we ordered Pepsi and fries. At times, we had to pool our money so that each person would get an equal share.

Hardly a day went by when I didn't think of the hardship on my parents of having four of us siblings away in learning institutions. Few families could have afforded such an expense; I wasn't totally convinced that they weren't eating peanut butter and jam sandwiches as they jokingly told us they did. I tried my best in terms of school work but the level of difficulty in some subjects was testing my resilience and endurance. In the end, I would succeed, but barely. I never did produce report cards that could have been framed. Thanks to the help and patience of the secular priests who doubled as teachers during the morning classes and tutors during the afternoon and evening study sessions, my grades were acceptable.

Although my spiritual advisor was Father Sirois, Father Allain, a much older priest, was my favourite. He came to my rescue a number of times. It was as if he could sense when things were getting out of hand. Contrary to the youthful good looking Father Sirois, Father Allain was probably in his late fifties. He was a tall, slender, grey-haired man with glasses, almost frail looking. We suspected that he had a touch of senility as he was beginning to lose his memory. Absent minded and aloof, he one day came to class and began to lecture; he was having a hard time getting our attention. We were trying hard not to laugh. He was wearing his pyjamas underneath his lab coat. He laughed it off and continued lecturing as if nothing was out of the ordinary.

A mere teenager, I started boarding school a few weeks before my 14th birthday. We were nine students in the grade 10 class. The dormitories were set up for maximum class sizes of 16. With more beds than students, we had more options for selecting bed locations. I chose the end unit closest to the washroom. Across the aisle from me was my nemesis by the name of Robert. We were total opposites in every way. What he liked, I disliked; where he excelled, I performed poorly. We were different in size, shape and height. He came from a political family, the son of a mayor of a small town; he was a neglected kid who got his way with everybody, typically those whom he bullied. From the start, he had decided that I would be his prime target. It was probably obvious that I could easily be manipulated given my small stature. Had he chosen the location of his bed to be close to me?

Curfew was at 9 p.m. which meant lights out. Each of us had to be in bed by that time. Father Allain or Father Ricardo would patrol the dormitories for about 30 minutes after the lights-out signal. Most of us knew that it was unwise to move or do anything that would bring attention to us. Robert waited. As soon as the coast was clear, though, he hissed at me and insisted that I come over to his bed. I was being forced into doing things I really did not want to do. I knew that if I didn't comply, he would certainly hit me or call me names in front of everyone else. I had no intention of telling anyone let alone one of the priests as I didn't want to get into trouble. Not only did I hate this pompous guy, I was mortified that I would be accused of initiating these nocturnal encounters. Could other boys hear us? Did they know what was happening to me? Would someone squeal? Would one of the priests patrolling the dormitories catch us in the act?

I tried hard not to dwell on these horrible incidents preferring to take advantage of the terrific schooling we were getting. Culturally, we were being exposed to all forms of art, architecture, photography and performing arts. Sharply at 7 a.m. every morning, we started the day with classical music. It lasted 30 minutes which allowed us enough time to wash up, get dressed and make our beds. At first, I didn't take too kindly to all this new music. For me, some of it was rather annoying. On Fridays, the selections were mostly upbeat, taken from the best of popular folk or traditional singers. I'm not in Dalhousie anymore, I would think to myself. I wanted out and I got out. Now was the time to open up to anything foreign to the closed-in environment of my hometown.

One day in early October, I came back to the dormitory to find all of Robert's belongings packed in boxes. Word was out that he had been expelled but nobody was suggesting why his precipitated departure had been so sudden. My lips were sealed; I would not talk about him or anything that had occurred between us.

A few days later, Father Allain asked me to come to his office. By this time, I knew he had found out what had being going on in the grade 10 dormitory. Had he witnessed it himself and decided not to embarrass me? Regardless of how he found out, he handled the situation in the kindest way possible. He closed the door, sat me down on a chair close to him and said, 'Are your problems over?'

'Yes Father,' I replied. 'You have no idea how relieved I am.'

'Say no more,' he said. 'How about coming with me to Grand Anse? I have to visit my mother... I would enjoy your company.'

Just as he said the word 'mother,' I had visions of my Mom finding out about the issues with Robert. How could she ever find out? There were only three people who knew for sure what had happened: Robert, Father Allain and me. It was a safe bet that the story would be kept a secret. I knew that Father Allain's invitation to go to Grand Anse was sincere; he just wanted me to feel safe again. I trusted him as much as he trusted me and for the next two years I felt the warmth of his security around me.

17

Travel as Far as the Eye Can See

'How is your Mom enjoying her retirement?' Norman said.

'I really don't know. We haven't spoken since mid June. I'm sure she's happy to be home with my father; he has been retired for two years already,' I said.

'What will she do in her sunset years?' he enquired.

'That's a good question. She loves to knit, play cards, do crossword puzzles and read. Will that be enough to fill her days? I do hope that she and my Dad find things to do together. Since my Dad quit work, he has done very little other than read newspapers and watch television. Mother, on the other hand, will not be happy just sitting around the house. Volunteering might appeal to her; I should mention it during the weekend,' I said.

'Well, my Mom seems quite content in Ottawa but she does miss the 'North Shore'. For the time being, she has her own apartment which she has decorated tastefully. Every couple of days, she comes by with homemade pies, cookies or soup,' he said.

'You are lucky to have your Mom so close that you can spend quality time with her often,' I said. 'Then again, I'm sure it can infringe on your personal time. It's nice that your Mom has met all of your friends; in fact, she was telling me that she does house cleaning for some of them.'

'Can you imagine a woman of her age still wanting to work so hard?' he said. 'She needs the money, I know, but there are easier jobs to be had.'

Life had never been easy for Norman's Mom. She has had to work hard all of her life. Now getting on in years with only a small government pension, she had little choice but to work to earn some extra cash. It was such a difference with my Mom who was starting her retirement with a good teacher's pension. How I admire the folks who do what they must. With a bit of luck, my parents would settle easily into the twilight years enjoying their hard-earned rest. Travel, not affordable while raising a family, could soon become a favourite pastime.

Travel had become quite a passion for me over the years. After my years in Dalhousie, I was eager to see the world. No place was too far or too foreign. Our yearly family trips to different parts of New Brunswick or Quebec had been a teaser. The more I saw and experienced, the more I wanted to go further afield. If travel is a good way to learn, then I'm the perfect student. I can thank my mother for that.

'Isn't this view of Rimouski just breathtaking?' I said. 'Unlike Dalhousie where the town is built on a steep hill, the streets of Rimouski are like soft waves mirroring the waves of the St. Lawrence Seaway'.

With the sail boats going in all directions in the late afternoon sun, and the light hitting the colourful sails, it is like the twinkling of lights on a Christmas tree. The air is pure yet it has that unmistakable taste of salt that you get close to the

Seaway. It was here that we came, from time to time, to shop for out-of-the-ordinary items that would have been difficult if not impossible to find in Dalhousie. It is also here that my mother's childhood friend, Roma, lived. Her yearly Christmas cards were always special. I met her only once when I was a young boy. Driving through Rimouski, I was reminded of her and her relationship with my mother. Some day, I hope to find the time to stop and visit with her.

I went on to tell Norman about my trip to Montreal in 1967. I had plans to attend Expo 67 and had made all the arrangements for accommodations with the Desrochers family (formerly from Dalhousie) living in Lachine at the time. Knowing how much it meant to me, my parents reluctantly agreed to this trip. Within weeks of my departure, my sister Claire announced that she too was going to Montreal and had plans to stay in a convent on Gouin Boulevard. My mother suggested that, if possible, we should stay at the same place. In the end, Clare and I did the whole trip together. It was at the Expo Theatre that I witnessed an early performance by 'The Supremes'. No words could ever describe how I felt at the time. Tickets for this coveted event were fetching top dollars on the day of the performance. My balcony seat was so far from the main stage that I could barely see the performers. That hardly mattered to me; just being there was the highlight of the trip.

'What is it about travel that you like so much?' Norman asked.

I pondered the question for what seemed like an eternity. Was it getting away from familiar surroundings or seeing new places? Was it because I could be myself without fear? He waited patiently for an answer that never came.

18

Around the Gaspé Coast

Look Ma'am, the price is almost the same. Do you want three beds, four?' the motel owner asked. 'I haven't got all night. These rooms will be rented by 5 p.m. so you need to decide soon. I've given you my best price... take it or leave it!'

Few people would bargain the way my mother did. Even when it came to buying a car, my father stood aside as my mother talked her way into some terrific deals. When we were on holidays, travelling as a family, we had front row seats to witness mother's negotiating skills.

These yearly holidays were never long but my memories of them are vivid. Dad would arrive from work and tell my mother that we would be leaving in a day or two. He had to plan his time off between the sailing of a ship and the docking of another. No advance reservations were made. Mother had probably formed a general idea of where we should go and what we might see, but these thoughts were kept to herself—probably so that we wouldn't get overly excited.

Money was always a big concern; mother always found ways to cut costs by packing as much food and beverages as we could store in the car. Picnic stops were the norm. Carefully choosing an interesting location, mother would quickly give orders so that meal preparation time was kept to a minimum. Soup would be heated and coffee made on a Coleman stove. From the cooler, we would take out cold beverages. Canned meats and other non perishables would be retrieved from a small box stowed in the trunk of the car.

It wouldn't be far off the mark to say that I felt privileged; many other families of similar means did not take annual trips the way we did. Ever the teacher, Mom would take advantage of these outings to bring us to historical landmarks and explain their significance. She insisted on pointing out to us incredible vistas, beautiful architecture, local customs, regional flora and fauna and buildings erected by or for Catholics. Acting as our private tour guide, whatever information she had gathered she shared with us before and during the trip.

One of the best memories I have is a boat tour around Percé Rock, towards the southern tip of the Gaspé Peninsula. A black and white picture of Ernie, Goeff and me all huddled at the rear of the small vessel was taken by my mother. In the background, you can see the majestic Percé Rock with its large hole allowing sea water to flow from one side to the other as sea gulls fly in every direction. Up close, their nesting grounds are highly visible. From the extreme end of the rock looking towards the mainland, one can distinguish that, at some point, the rock was carved out of the mainland by the incessant waves. The picture shows us without life jackets which were not mandatory in those days. Although I was not a swimmer, I wasn't afraid of being on this small tourist boat which would not have been very secure had the weather turned bad. The only saving grace was that we weren't too far from shore.

'Do you see those outdoor ovens?' Mom said.

'Where, I don't see them,' I said.

'There is one in front of almost every house,' she said. 'They bake bread in them and sell them to passers-by. I think we'll stop and get a loaf or two.'

Construction of these ovens varied from one house to the other. Some were built right on the ground. Others were built-up on a pedestal making it easier to access the bread and to stoke the fire. Regardless of the shape or construction, all of them were white - either painted or covered with lime; I never did find out which.

As the years went on, the frequency of these family trips diminished; they were always, in my opinion the highlight of summer if not of the whole year. In a way, my prayers had been answered; I had been able to get out of the lousy town and see the world. Those wonderful get-aways would prove to be the start of my travel bug.

19

Montreal Madness

'We should be getting close to Ste Flavie by now,' I said.

'Yes, we should be there very soon,' Norman said. 'That's where we leave the St Lawrence Seaway.' Then turning inland they drove towards Mont Joli, Amqui, Causapscal and finally to the banks of the beautiful Matapédia River. The rolling hills green with pastures, pristine homes and cattle barns dotted the landscape as far as the eye could see. I love this part of the trip.'

'All of this reminds me of our overnight train trips from Campbellton to Montreal,' I said.

'I had almost forgotten about those expeditions we did in the early seventies,' Norman said.

'How could you forget?' I said. 'The fun we had on those Canadian National trains; we hardly slept a wink, we were so excited about going to the big city. I remember pooling our money so that we could stretch the dollars as much as possible. Once in Montreal, we spent like mad the first few days leaving us short of cash for the final days and the return trip. Part of the fun was making ends meet—which we always did. We'd come back to the old town with new fashions from the big city that were sure to have people laugh at us and call us names such as fags, queers, and sissies.'

In those days, a person could get a reasonable room in downtown Montreal at the YMCA. The added advantage was that you could meet other interesting people. Norman was never very shy about meeting new people and soon after our arrival he would disappear for hours on end. On a few occasions, we only saw him the next morning. When meeting at the YMCA cafeteria after a night out on the town, the stories were incredible; we heard first-hand accounts of his exploits such as who he met in the bars, where they went and what they did. A story teller extraordinaire, Norman would provide all the details of his adventures leaving nothing to the imagination. The more surprised we were, the more he added to the stories which were in part fabricated to entertain us.

Not far from the YMCA on Stanley Street were a number of small but good disco bars where the music was perfect for dancing. Dave, Norman and I would arrive in one of these bars far too early but because the music was so great, we would stay and party to the wee hours before making it back to the YMCA long after the doors had been locked for the night. We'd ring the door bell, identify ourselves by name and room number, and then enter as the door magically opened without any human assistance.

20

An Unusual Christmas

To a Catholic family, Christmas and Easter are high holy days. Christmas in our family was steeped in tradition taken from both sides of the family. The Acadian traditions came from my mother's family. As my father had been born in the United States, we kept some American traditions alive. My father would secure a Christmas tree just days prior to the big day and store it in the back yard or on the front veranda until it was time to bring it in. So as to not excite us too much, the tree was taken indoors around the 23rd of December which left very little time to decorate it. Placed in a pail full of potatoes to ensure that it would stand straight and not keel over, the tree was trimmed with multi-coloured lights, Christmas ornaments and tinsel. An angel was placed at the top of the tree and a *crèche* beneath it. The sofa was moved slightly to the right and the stereo cabinet a tad to the left to allow room for the tree to stand in the corner.

Late on Christmas Eve, my mother would take out her usual candy treats and put them in the living and dining rooms. There were always a bowl of nuts in the shell, barley toy candies, chicken bone candies, humbugs, ribbon candy, hard candies and liquorice candies. The house was decorated the same way every year. Bells and make-believe holly would be hung from the light fixture in the front hall. A plastic red wreath with a candle and a red light acting as the flame were hung in each of the four front windows of the house; two upstairs in the front bedrooms and two downstairs in the living room windows. A red and black square candle imitating a chimney would sit in the centre of the coffee table. A set of outdoor lights would be strung on a tree or around a bush near the front door.

Families came together at Christmas; it was tradition. I felt close to my siblings and my parents at this time of the year. It was a favourite time for many reasons: I enjoyed the music both sacred and secular; I loved the traditional dishes and desserts; I enjoyed giving and receiving gifts; I liked the pageantry of midnight mass at church; I fancied the holiday decorations and, most of all, I took great pleasure in seeing relatives and friends even though some of them stayed only for a short visit as they were making the rounds of all the people they knew.

In one of the many photographs taken at Christmas time, I'm sitting in front of the tree with my brothers Geoff and Ernie. I'm wearing a white dress shirt and dark pants while my brothers are in pyjamas; all three of us are waiting to be given the signal that we can open gifts. The reason I'm not in pyjamas is that I had attended midnight mass where I had performed 'Silent Night' on the church organ. Sister Angelina, who taught piano lessons at the St. John Bosco School, thought that it would be nice if a few of her students could showcase their talents in front of the whole community. This was a happy occasion for me and a proud one for my family.

In those days, when it came time for Communion, the members of the church choir along with the organist would make their way down to the main level and proceed to the front of the church. They would be the first at the communion rail to receive Holy Communion so that they could go back to the loft and sing. Once back in formation, they started to entertain the faithful with a few sacred carols. My turn came after the third carol. Hardly reaching the pedals, I sat upright with pride and joy. The notes came easily but nerves had affected me up until I reached the end at which point I felt a ton of bricks had been taken off my shoulders. It was all over in a matter of minutes. Returning to my assigned seat not far from the organist, I felt a bit more relaxed as I started to settle down. Streams of people were still lined up for Holy Communion—it seemed to go on and on. I watched with interest to see the people I knew. Some of the ladies observing me from below managed a small wave to acknowledge my presence. Boy did that feel good! My parents were in the church that night to hear me play. At the end of Mass, they left before I did and got home just as I arrived.

'Did you go to Communion?' mother asked.

'Oh my God,' I replied, 'I completely forgot. I was so nervous about playing the organ, it never occurred to me that I should have joined the choir members and gone to Holy Communion before the congregation did.'

'Well, you'll just have to get up for the 10 a.m. mass so that you don't miss Holy Communion on Christmas Day,' mother said.

This did not sit well with me but what other choice did I have?

Of all the family traditions I enjoyed, anything having to do with food was at the top my list. Our annual family traditions started with my mother's version of 'chicken fricot,' an Acadian dish that is somewhere between a soup and a stew made with chicken, potatoes, onions, carrots, turnip in a light broth with plenty of savoury. This was served as the evening meal on Christmas Eve. In the early years, we were put to bed at about 8:30 p.m. and told that we would be awakened after midnight mass at about 1.30 a.m. Then the fun started.

As soon as my parents returned from Midnight Mass, my mother would prepare a lunch in the French Canadian tradition. The *réveillon* consisted of a light meal which always included Christmas desserts. Every year, Mom made meat pies in early December which were stored in the freezer; two of these pies would be taken out and heated in the oven while we opened gifts.

I felt a bit odd not being in pyjamas as I would normally have been, but I was certainly proud that I had been given the opportunity to play music in public. My grandmother, a fervent Catholic, was most certainly overjoyed about her grandson's accomplishment. From Christmas photos taken that year she is seen dressed from head to toe in black as a sign of mourning for my grandfather who had passed away a year before.

The party went on for a few hours as relatives from both sides of my family popped in to wish us Merry Christmas. Some of them joined us for the night-time meal. Both the kitchen table and the dining-room table would be set-up to seat as many people as required. Mom's best Old English Rose china and Lady Hamilton silverware were used on these special occasions. Pickles and homemade cranberry sauce were always on hand as they were favourite accompaniments for the delicious meat pies. Desserts always included fruit cake (Mom made both a light and dark fruit cake), scotch cookies (with icing and a half of a red or green glazed cherry on top), mocha balls (small cubes of pound cake coated in icing and covered in either crushed peanuts or coconut), gum drop cake, cherry almond cake, lemon loaf and assorted cookies from recipes taken out of Chatelaine or Reader's Digest.

'Don't forget to put the alarm clock on,' Mom said as I went up the stairs to the boys' bedroom. 'You need to go to mass in the morning!'

'I know, I know,' I said.

I was hoping to get out of that but my very devout mother would make sure that I would not go against church law for fear of excommunication, I'm sure. Or perhaps, was it that she feared what *her* mother would say to her if, per chance, I missed Mass on a High Holy Day. Both my grandparents were staunch Catholics; they were amongst the group of families who had founded the parish. Following church law was paramount; any deviations would be dealt with severely. Although my grandfather died when I was 10 years old, I still remember the day he caught me coming out of the woods behind our house, on the feast on the Immaculate Conception. I was hauling Christmas trees I intended to sell to make a tidy profit; he was furious with me, but I think my mother got the brunt of it. I had learned a valuable lesson I was not about to forget: if you want respect from your elders, don't work on high holy days.

From year to year, Christmas was essentially the same. The house was decorated with the identical ornaments which my father had retrieved from the attic. Mom's Christmas baking was repeated every year with a few additions for the sake of variety. At times, visitors to our home included people from out of town visiting for the holidays.

During one particularly rough winter, one of the ships in port was not able to return to England, leaving the crew to spend Christmas in Dalhousie. My father invited the captain and the 1st engineer to have Christmas dinner with our family. Happy to be able to get off the ship and into a family environment, they readily accepted the invitation. As a token of their appreciation, they brought a bottle of rum for my father and a box of Quality Street chocolates from England for my mother. And so began a long tradition of having Quality Street chocolates at Christmas time.

It wasn't often that I had a chance to observe foreigners; this golden opportunity allowed me to listen to the stories of these two gentlemen talking about their lives and family back in England. Speaking in the Queen's English, I marvelled at their ability to string sentences together and their use of appropriate vocabulary. Refined and sophisticated, they were impeccably dressed and had aristocratic manners. By the time they left the house, I was completely under their spell. The elegant tin of

Quality Street chocolates was kept long after the contents had disappeared. To our surprise, the following year, another tin of Quality Street chocolates was delivered to our house just before Christmas. In those days, these delicacies were not available in Canada; we felt quite honoured to be given Quality Street chocolates every year.

21

Our Favourite Librarian

Do you remember Garry Chong, the town's assistant librarian in the late sixties?' I said.

'Difficult to forget.' Norman answered.

'I wonder whatever became of him.' I said. 'After he left Dalhousie, we never heard from him again although the librarian thought that he was living not far from Toronto and had married a Chinese girl.'

'What would possess someone to come from Taiwan to Dalhousie?' Norman mused.

'From what I know, he came to Canada to study library sciences and following his degree, he was offered a position at the new Dalhousie Centennial Library,' I said.

For a young man, Garry was much more mature than we were, as high school students, at the time. He had his own apartment on Adelaide Street which was always open to us regardless of the day or time we visited. Offering a bowl of rice, he would listen to our stories and give us some sound advice which wasn't always what we wanted to hear. From an educated background, his father a doctor and his mother a nurse, Garry offered us a glimpse of another culture we hardly knew. His command of the English language was phenomenal although his pronunciation was a bit odd at times. My best recollection comes from a day in late September when he came into the apartment saying, 'I just put the 'crows' on the 'crows line'. He had hung bed sheets to dry on the clothes line.

Garry was a mentor to me; for that I will always be thankful. Not long after arriving in Dalhousie, he met Larry, an executive at the paper mill. They became friends. Larry also became a friend of *mine* during my high school years. The connection between Garry, Larry and me became stronger over time as we shared our highs and lows of living in Dalhousie. Larry would move away but would eventually return as both he and his wife had family in our community.

On a typical Friday or Saturday night, we would convene at Garry's apartment. It was a tiny arrangement with a minuscule kitchen and small living room on the ground floor. A very narrow staircase led to the bedroom loft. It wasn't unusual to have 5 to 6 of us show up at Garry's door on a weekend night to enjoy each other's company. It didn't take very long before wagging tongues started rumours about us. All of this reached the ears of Garry's landlady, an elderly spinster not keen on having anyone tarnish her good reputation. For a while, we avoided visiting Garry, preferring instead to meet elsewhere so that we would not jeopardize his inexpensive and convenient accommodations.

We were never sure of exactly what people imagined was happening in that apartment to cause them to make false accusations about us. Although alcohol was consumed on the premises from time to time, it was kept to a minimum. Most of our evenings were spent talking about current events, cultural happenings, anticipated travel and plans for the future.

In such a small town, cultural outlets were few. One saving grace was the Cultural Society of the Baie des Chaleurs. Every year, they brought in high-quality talent chosen from a very broad range of musical taste. People showing interest in cultural events were considered high brow. However, that did not stop any of us from attending these inspirational performances. My mother and several of her friends were members of the Society, thus allowing me an opportunity to buy tickets to see some of the coveted shows. Men who liked this kind of entertainment were deemed 'queer'. I hated the fact that if you liked art or music, people assumed that you were gay. And it was equally upsetting to me that my Mother associated being gay to being a pervert which I certainly wasn't.

Some of the concerts I attended were world class; they included, for example, performances by Monique Leyrac and *les*

Compagnons de la chanson. The performers were not always well known but certainly the music they played was. One concert featured 'Duo Harpists'; two rather effeminate men each playing a harp with perfect synchronisation. They commented rather humorously that they were 'harpists' and not 'harpies' which garnered howls of laughter from the audience. In attendance that evening at the Campbellton High School Auditorium, were some well known gay men from Campbellton. One of them, the husband of a prolific painter, approached my mother and asked her. 'Are you Charles' mother?' I was not within hearing distance of this interchange which occurred at intermission, as Norman and I had decided to go outdoors for fresh air. At the end of the show, my mother, her friend Diane, Norman and I piled into the car for the drive back to Dalhousie. On the way home, out of the blue, my mother said, 'Charles, I hope you're not following in Tony's footsteps'. Silence is golden I said to myself; there was no point in commenting on the remark. For the next ten minutes, the sounds of silence were deafening. Fearing the continuation of the discussion which would likely follow at home in private, I was relieved that my mother never again brought up the subject. I am not sure of exactly what I would have said to her but I certainly would have made the point that I had no intention of imitating Tony who was married and running around town trying to coerce any young guy in spending time with him.

22

Returning to Notre Dame High School

In the hallways of the Notre Dame High School, students milled around waiting for the first morning bell to ring. Some were already seated at their desk in the homeroom while others were moving slowly, talking to buddies and making plans for recess. Although I had been a student in this same building in the 9th grade, I was now a senior making a comeback to Dalhousie after being away for two years and experiencing life in a boarding school. I felt out of place, out of sync with other classmates who seemed to know what was going on, who was dating who and how to avoid staying out of trouble. It was my first day back in this learning environment that would prove to be very difficult for me to adjust, not because of school subjects but because of my feelings towards life in general. Some of the familiar faces seemed friendly enough for me to go forward and say 'Hi, I'm back!' Others looked at me rather inquisitively wondering where I came from. I hadn't arrived at school in a yellow bus and therefore I wasn't from the outskirts.

My homeroom, in the west wing of the building, was right across from another classroom of grade 12 students except that the front of our room was right across from the back of their classroom. Each classroom had two doors with glass panels; one at the front of the room and one towards the back. I chose a desk in the last row along the windows and squarely in front of the homeroom teacher's desk. At that point, I had no idea who the homeroom teacher would be. Looking around the room, I noticed a few girls sitting next to me who obviously wanted to get to know me. I introduced myself and within minutes I had the full description of Bill, our homeroom teacher that had all the girls gaga over him. When he did finally come into the room, I understood why. A tall lanky man in his late forties with just a touch of grey hair, Bill's eyes were his trademark; one was grey green and the other was grey. Based on my quick assessment, I knew we would get along well.

From my seat during the next twenty minutes that it took to get settled, I could see students in the room across the hall seated in the back rows. I spotted a young man with a well-cropped beard. From my vantage point, he appeared stunning. I made a mental note to find out more about him at recess.

Bill, our homeroom teacher, took attendance and answered questions from several of my classmates. When the bell rang at the end of the 10 minute homeroom time, the day began with a history class for which Bill was the assigned teacher. Fifty minutes later, the bell rang to signal the end of the first period and the start of the next period: math taught by Sister Johanna. Dressed in a modified nun's habit with a skirt to her knees and not to the ankles as we had seen in previous years, she spent the entire period setting the ground rules for her classes. Profanities and rude behaviour would not be tolerated in the least. She expected us to act like the adults we were, on the verge of going off to university. Her old fashioned approach was genuine; how could anyone fault her for wanting decency. The first segment of the day was over; it was time for morning recess.

Dressed in very fashionable clothing, Dave, a tall dark-haired youth with small brown eyes and a mischievous smile, also in Grade 12, greeted me in the school yard in a manner that showed interest and respect; we shared the same math teacher but not the same homeroom. He would become one of my most trusted friends and together we would spend a lot of our free time together in our last year of schooling in Dalhousie. Over the course of twelve months, I came to know his parents who were so supportive of him and so caring to me. Kindred spirits we were but cautious all the while not to alarm others to the fact that we were different from the norm and could easily have been the target of bullying. I enquired about the bearded wonder across the hall from my homeroom. He had also noticed 'Johnny' but knew very little about him except that he lived with his family in Jacquet River, some 30 miles east of town.

The year was 1969; the Prime Minister of our country had said publicly that the nation had no business in the bedrooms of Canadians. Hailed as a breakthrough, Dave, Norman and I rejoiced on the day of this pronouncement but kept our reactions very private. In those days, one did not talk about sexual orientation very openly. Few people knew that Dave was seeing a married man by the name of Homer. Fewer people still would have understood the strong bond that united them. Part of me felt that this relationship was inappropriate but how could I possibly condemn love between two consenting adults? I was envious of them but not to the point of wanting to start a relationship for the sake of doing so. Norman was also envious but his reasons were different. He had been Homer's special friend before he introduced him to Dave. Betrayed by Dave, Norman nevertheless believed that one should never regret anything and never keep a grudge; it was good experience, as Edith Piaf sang so confidently: *'Non, rien de rien, non, je ne regrette rien, ni le bien qu'on m'a fait, ni le mal, tout ça m'est bien égal...'*

Planning started early for the Year Book and graduation activities. These rituals had escaped me during my years in an all-boys boarding school but quickly came back into full focus at Dalhousie. The accoutrements surrounding this rite of passage included a new suit for graduation day and the gala that followed. Needing a partner for the evening, I asked Monique if she would accompany me. From a large family with very limited income, she had found part-time employment as a baby sitter for one of the high school teachers. Her meagre earnings were still enough to purchase a steel blue taffeta gown that made her look like she was part of a royal family. Dave and Norman also found willing young ladies who dressed the part but knew that this was a one-evening affair. We suspected that these two girls were secretly in love with each other. On the dance floor, the six of us made quite an impression. We were all suspect in the eyes of the other young men and women but our time in Dalhousie was coming to an end, allowing us to feel a bit freer with our emotions.

Dave had been accepted at the Université de Moncton and was planning to major in Biology. Norman was uncertain about his future but had thought about becoming a hairdresser. My mind had been made up just after seeing a school guidance counsellor who had told me that my strength was in the area of interior design. At the time, the only institution offering a degree program was the University of Manitoba. To be accepted, one had to have Grade 13. That meant that I had to complete one year in university before I could consider going to Winnipeg, so I chose St. Thomas University in Fredericton. All three of us would be staying in New Brunswick, allowing us to visit each other or at least to see each other in Dalhousie during holidays.

'You know, Norman, I felt bad leaving you in Dalhousie when we went off to university, Dave and I,' I said, 'felt that we were abandoning you at a time when you would need the comfort of good friends to survive the macho and anti-gay environment of small-town Canada.'

'I stayed in part because of my Mother,' he said. 'I knew she needed me and I was ready to stay for a while. But after almost a year, I needed to learn a trade so I decided that I would follow my dream and study hairdressing. The O'Neil School of Hair Design in Saint John was my preferred choice. My Aunt Bea was so excited at the possibility that I would be moving to her town that she immediately offered to have me stay with her on Orange Street.'

'How different our journeys have been,' I said. 'Yet, our mothers have been the central figure in our lives. Dominant and authoritarian, both wanted the best for their children even if it meant us going away to obtain what was not locally available—be it jobs, education, training or exposure to other spheres of life. Wanting to become an interior designer did not exactly please my mother any more than hairdressing impressed yours. In those days, mostly women worked in these professions and the few men that did, had a sordid reputation, warranted or not. I was aware of that at the time but nothing would stop me from following my dream.'

23

Career Choices

The trip to Dalhousie always seemed longer than the return back to Ottawa; this time was no exception. Our conversations were mostly short as neither of us wanted to disturb the other. We seldom talked politics, not having much interest in that subject. But the election of John Turner would have given us fodder for a healthy debate. We wondered about Mr. Turner's readiness to assume the leadership of our country; not that our nation was going through difficult times but there was a feeling that the world, as a whole, was facing unprecedented events. These included a host of catastrophes such as the famine affecting nearly 10 million people in Ethiopia, the killing of 3,500 people as a result of a gas leak at the Union Carbide pesticide plant in Bhopal, India, and the massacre of 20 people at a McDonald's restaurant on July 18th in San Ysidro, California.

Seventeen years after our centennial in 1967, Canada was still regarded as one of the best countries in the world. Nearly seventy banks closed in the United States in 1984, but in our country, things were rather stable. The only fly in the ointment was the discovery of AIDS. Knowing very little about the disease, most gay men in my circle of friends were concerned about the physical and emotional effects on the guys who had already been diagnosed. Here and there were horror stories of a person getting ill almost overnight! My friend Mike had told me of a case in New York City where a man was diagnosed with AIDS on a Friday and died before the weekend was over. Haunting images of people in excruciating pain were beginning to surface.

Death and dying were not topics that held my attention for very long. At 32 years of age, in perfect health, I spent precious little time worrying about my final days. Although aware that one hangs on to life by a thread, my only health concerns were linked to my arthritis. It had been getting worse in recent years but people didn't die from this painful condition. It was simply a cross to bear, one that I knew I would deal with increasingly in the years to come. A legacy from my mother's gene pool, I had inherited ankylosing spondylitis, a form of rheumatoid arthritis which causes inflammation primarily in the groin and the lower back and often leads to a fusion of disks in the spine. That my mother and I had the same condition was certainly part of our strong bond;

however, I prayed that I would never be subject to the intensity of pain she had experienced most of her life. I had been aware that on difficult days, to get to her classroom, she would walk along the wall and steady herself to avoid a fall. On many days, the pain was apparent on her face washing away her usual smile and replacing it with a sadness that went straight to my heart.

24

University 101

Because I had chosen to work towards a university degree, my mother could not suggest that it was inappropriate from the standpoint of education but she tried, as best she could, to point out that life for me in this interior design profession could be miserable... something she would not want for any of her sons.

While Norman went on to study in his chosen trade, I was busy doing courses that would amount to the equivalent of Grade 13. St. Thomas University was a whole new world for me, offering all kinds of subjects I knew nothing about. Situated in the heart of Fredericton, the capital city of the province, the campus grounds included the University of New Brunswick faculties and the new Teacher's College. The architectural style of the buildings was similar to an Ivy League campus where the use of red bricks and beige trim bring all of the elements together and create a sense of order and symmetry. It conveyed a feeling of trust in these educational institutions.

With easy access to downtown and to the new uptown where a shopping centre had opened, the opportunities to escape were numerous. It was tempting to skip class to go shopping or just to walk around in the historic part of town and admire all the beautiful Victorian homes. Founded as Fort St. Anne, the city of Fredericton was smaller than Moncton and Saint John; still it offered everything that the larger centres provided.

Room 117 in Harrington Hall was my home during my time at St. Thomas. I shared the tiny room with Jack, a native of the Miramichi region who had relatives living near Dalhousie. We had little in common other than being men; he had his group of buddies, mostly drinking buddies. The smell of liquor permeated our room quite often as he would get in late at night, three sheets to the wind. He was a good person, and although he never studied very hard, he had good grades. That's more than I could say for myself.

Alone and without much guidance, I made my course selection based on my limited knowledge of the fields of study offered. In retrospect, I should have obtained much more information before making these critical decisions that would eventually haunt me. I chose poorly, with negative consequences. I struggled in Math but to no avail. I did better in Economics but not enough to get a pass. Philosophy was not much better although I did find the subject matter very interesting, but my efforts were not to the level required to get a passing grade. To my horror, the year ended in complete failure such that going to the University of Manitoba was out of the question. How could I have been so naive to think that things would fall into place and that I would be enrolled in the Bachelor of Interior Design program?

The shock of not getting what I had hoped for was my first major blow. I think that my mother must have been happy that my firm plans for interior design school were down the drain though she said nothing about it to me.

'You'll find other things to do with your life; don't dwell on it,' she said.

With no career in sight, no plans for continuing education, my only option was to go back home to Dalhousie. Keeping a low profile, I did my best to find suitable employment as fast as I could. I thought of becoming a flight attendant which fitted neatly with my desire to travel. I pursued that goal without success. A local job advertisement led to an interview with the Canadian Imperial Bank of Commerce (CIBC) in another city. This first business trip of my career was at once scary and uplifting. I had no idea what to expect yet the paid trip to a large city was a big bonus for me. Halifax, at the time, was booming and although I was there in late fall long after the tourists had left this port city, it gave me confidence to think that business people wanted to talk to me about a career in their organization. I don't recall much of the interview but I must have made a half-decent impression as I got a call two days after I returned to Dalhousie. They were offering a management trainee position in the university town of Antigonish, Nova Scotia. I was assigned a position at the CIBC campus branch in the Student Union Building. Although I had never been to that town, I knew about it as my oldest brother had graduated from St. Francis Xavier University, a few years earlier.

To make my transition easier, bank officials had arranged for temporary accommodation in a private residence. It was in the early days of February 1972 that I arrived by train in this small community just a few short miles from the entrance to Cape Breton Island. I lived with an elderly couple at 40 St. Mary's Street, a short walk from the campus. Room and board was reasonable and the McNaughtons were a friendly, religious couple. They rented out two of the three bedrooms on the second floor of their tiny house. In the other rented room were two Royal Canadian Mounted Police (RCMP) officers who looked at me rather strangely.

I wanted to be feel at home in my new environment so I integrated as quickly as I could. The university campus was a great place to meet and make new friends. Through contacts made at the bank, I got invited to parties held in rooms at the student residences. In a matter of a month, I had made a new circle of friends some of whom are still in the picture forty years later. One such person was Shane who visited me on St. Mary's Street. His fondness for the music of Mireille Mathieu struck me as being rather odd as he spoke no French and understood very little of the language. In my room, we would listen to her music; I would translate the meaning of the songs. For the two RCMP officers in the next room, my musical preferences and choice of friends were suspect. They made their feelings known to Mrs. McNaughton who immediately protected me by saying that she was sure nothing inappropriate was going on in my room. She was furious with them; not long after that incident, the officers moved out.

25

Getting Closer

We are within two hundred miles from home,' I said. 'The Matapédia Valley is one part of this long journey that I enjoy. Even though the road is very windy, the river below with all the salmon fishermen either standing in knee high water or in small boats is always a treat to see. Every year, people from over the North America fly into this area—one of the best for Atlantic salmon fishing.'

'Just imagine the money that comes as a result of this industry!' Norman said.

'There's not much here to attract outsiders but surely, the beauty of this part of Canada must impress people who have never been here before,' I said.

'If only the winters weren't so long and cold,' Norman said.

'By the time it gets warm enough for tourists to want to come to Northern New Brunswick and the Gaspé Peninsula, the high season is well underway in other parts of the land,' I said. 'Our window of opportunity is so short; a mere 4 to 6 weeks at best.'

'Travelling during the Labour Day weekend is always difficult with so many people on the road,' Norman said. 'Any plans for the weekend?'

His question remained unanswered while I wondered what reaction I would get arriving home unannounced. Not that my parents needed a warning. They would likely be sitting in the living room, Dad reading the newspaper and Mom working on a crossword puzzle or doing yoga. The family home, a two-story wooden structure designed in large part by my father, was purely utilitarian. Over the years, the exterior had been renovated by taking away my beloved front veranda and replacing it by a small wrought iron staircase and canopy. Much of the interior had remained the same over the years with one exception: new oak cupboards graced the kitchen walls, my mother's pride and joy. At the same time, a new kitchen floor had been laid and new appliances installed.

Growing up in a 1200 square foot house with only one bathroom was a challenge for a family of eight although we were seldom all at home at the same time. Of modest means, my parents saved money before spending it. My Dad insisted that the house be completely paid off before he would consider purchasing a vehicle. He was quite content to walk to work even in the coldest days of winter. Dressed with insulated underwear under his dark green work uniform and lunch box in hand, he would set out to walk the half-mile trek from our home to the wharf where he worked as a stevedore foreman.

I knew that when I would arrive, he would be sitting in the large arm chair which was reserved for him. We were allowed to sit in that chair only if he wasn't using it and we would be expected to find another seat if he entered the room and wanted it. My father had very few needs other than his chair and the television. He worked long hours which gave him very little rest time. Neither an avid reader nor a hobbyist, he preferred watching news and weather forecasts.

26

Failed Attempts

From Antigonish, Nova Scotia, the bank transferred me to Alberton, Prince Edward Island. I had to look on a map to find this town as I had never heard of it. With my meagre belongings which now included a sound system, I made the trip by bus. Again, bank officials had secured lodging for my first week. I lived with a family on a farm; however, they could not keep me on and I had to find another place. Word got out that I was looking to rent a room with kitchen facilities and within a short period of time, I moved to a new location in a very old house.

As much as I had wanted to see the world, I was not that keen on spending much time in Alberton which, at the time, was home to about 700 people. During my fifth week, I requested and obtained a transfer. My next destination was Campbellton, a mere skip and a jump from Dalhousie, a place I knew very well. I wasn't too thrilled about going back to the North Shore but I could sense that it wouldn't be for long.

My stint with the Canadian Imperial Bank of Commerce came to an abrupt end after I was called into the Manager's office and asked if it was true that I was interested in a career as a flight attendant with Air Canada. It would have been near impossible for me to lie, so I told the truth. It was explained to me that since I wasn't serious about becoming a bank manager, there was no sense investing in me and therefore I was being dismissed from my job effective that same business day. With no work and no income, I temporarily moved back to Dalhousie.

It had been almost a year since I had last left Dalhousie with no plans ever to go back there to live. Out of desperation, I applied for every advertised job that was posted in our local newspapers. Soon afterwards, I got a call from a representative of Irving Oil in the Campbellton office. My interview went well and within two days, I was called to a second interview to be held in Saint John. A quick call to Norman and I secured accommodations for the time I would be there to meet the Irving Oil officials. The meeting took place in a small boardroom on the fourth floor of the Golden Ball Building right across a very old cemetery in downtown Saint John. Evidently they were impressed enough to offer me a job in the accounting department although I had no real accounting experience with the exception of working in the banking industry. All I needed now was to find suitable permanent accommodations.

Upon finding out that I was coming to Saint John on a permanent basis, Norman asked his Aunt Bea if I could stay with them temporarily until I was able to find a room or small apartment. For the next eight months, I shared my life with Norman and his Aunt Bea in their ground floor three bedroom apartment on Orange Street. Norman had completed his training at a school of hair design and had also been offered permanent employment at that school. A relationship had begun between Norman and a guy by the name of Brent Barrett but by the time I had arrived it had cooled off. My presence was not appreciated by Brent as I was seen as an intruder. There was no love lost between Brent and I; I simply did not trust him and felt that he probably suffered from mental problems.

A few months after I had moved to Saint John, I met Douglas, an accountant from Montreal who had relocated to southern New Brunswick. He seemed familiar but I couldn't figure out if I had met him before or not. It turned out that he had worked for International Paper in their Head Office in Montreal and had been to Dalhousie along with two other colleagues to perform audits. They had stayed at the Cedar Lodge Motel where I worked; I had indeed met him before. Norman also knew one of these three guys as he had befriended Lewis Ladouceur.

Douglas and I hit if off well; we started seeing each other on a regular basis. Occasionally, I would spend the night with him in his apartment coming home to Orange Street in the morning. One Saturday morning, just as I was coming in, Bea had just gone out to walk the dog. Norman was standing in the vestibule waiting for a taxi to pick him up. With a stone face, he looked at me and said wryly, 'one bitch goes out and another one comes in'. It was so unexpected that on the spur of the moment I didn't have time to react. When he got back from work that evening, we went out for drinks at a local bar. We laughed all the way there repeating the same phrase that had come out of his mouth so unexpectedly.

In the accounting department of Irving Oil, there were several divisions; I worked in the 'truck cost accounting'. Seated at desks arranged in the same manner as a classroom with no dividers between the workers, we tallied expenses incurred for the maintenance of each of the vehicles that were used to transport oil. The only equipment required was a calculator, the type that prints out the recorded figures on a narrow band of paper. There must have been around twenty of us all using our calculators at the same time making a sound quite similar to slot machines in a Casino. The sound was deafening, and not at all pleasant. Luckily, there were a few people working there who were very helpful and kind to me. Without them, I would have been completely lost. With constant encouragement and support, I was able to get through the long days. Deep inside, I knew this was not the place for me; it was a stepping stone, a time to recoup and decide what I would do next, what I wanted to do for the rest of my life.

The job with Irving Oil brought me very little satisfaction. What was a dyslexic person doing in an accounting job? I hated numbers; quite often, I would reverse digits making it impossible to balance. I was able to keep that job until the day I announced proudly that I would be returning to university in the Fall. My application had been accepted for the new 'translation and interpretation' program offered at the Université de Moncton.

My colleagues were elated. They knew that I needed to find myself. Irving Oil would not be where I would earn my living. As soon as I had told management that I was leaving, my co-workers organized a farewell party. For once, I was part of a group and felt accepted even though I was so different from most of them in the office. I was leaving on my own terms and not because I wasn't wanted or needed. That positive feeling helped me make the transition back to student life in a different university, in a different town.

27

Almost There

'Gosh Norman, it seems like it was only yesterday that I moved from Saint John to Moncton to go back to school,' I said.

'You left me alone again,' he said. 'After you were gone, my relationship with Brent went from bad to worse to the point that I had to leave town without a trace. I felt like a fugitive on the run packing my stuff in a few cardboard boxes and shipping them to Hull, Québec. For fear that Brent would take it out on Aunt Bea or force her to tell him where I had moved to, I didn't tell her where I was going. I took a late night flight for Ottawa arriving in the nation's capital in the wee hours of the morning.'

'Did you hear from him after your escape?' I said.

'Aunt Bea told me that he had called several times and had come to the apartment not believing that I was no longer there,' Norman said. 'A few years later, my mother sent me a clipping from the St. John Telegraph. In the article, I found out that Brent had been found dead behind an abandoned building. He was really strange, at times neurotic. Brent worked in a mental health institution; I often wondered if he himself had mental health issues. When we were watching television one night at his apartment, he took out a revolver from a drawer behind us and pointed it to my head saying *watch TV*. I presumed that the gun wasn't loaded although it was quite unnerving. I felt my life was in danger because of him; I needed to get out of there.'

'*Getting out of Dodge* seems to be a common theme between you and me,' I said.

Now out of the Matapédia Valley and closer to the New Brunswick border, we could see in the distance the silhouette of the Van Horne Bridge linking Cross Point and Campbellton. Nearing the Mi'kmac reservation, we could see the city lights of

Campbellton just ahead. Closer to the entrance of the bridge our eyes were drawn to the seedy remains of the motel and gas station where the Marie Antoinette restaurant had been. Memories of crossing the Restigouche River by ferry boat and going for a huge butterscotch sundae at Marie Antoinette's almost brought tears to my eyes. I thought about my cousin Mike with whom I had shared some wonderful moments as a young lad.

We drove through Campbellton slowly not because of the speed limit but because we wanted to look at all the old landmarks that brought back so many memories. We saw 'Le Chateau,' an old colonial-style hotel where Norman had once given me kissing lessons in a room rented by his mother. We drove by the Home Hardware where Homer had been a manager; Norman recalled the good times he had had with him before their relationship came to an abrupt end. On Water Street stood the old Canadian Imperial Bank of Commerce building which had closed years before.

Rather than take the divided highway that links Campbellton and Dalhousie, we opted for the old road that runs along the Restigouche. New houses had sprouted here and there while a few of the older homes appeared derelict. Some places never change; the Restigouche Golf and Country Club property was still well maintained. The CKNB radio station building was still standing; however, it appeared to have new tenants. Further down the road, we arrived at Dalhousie Junction where in the 1950's passengers on the Halifax-Montreal trains would stop and transfer to downtown Dalhousie. The CN station building had long been torn down when that service was cancelled.

A few minutes later, we drove past the O'Leary's Cedar Lodge Motel known for its thriving discothèque and intimate dining room with a view of the Restigouche. Norman's mother had worked there for a number of years and on occasion, he had helped serving tables for large weddings. My brother Phil had also worked there when he came back home from university for the summer months. I had worked there as well, as a summer student, for a couple of years. We reminisced about the good old days of working for the O'Leary family. It was a thriving business in its heyday; the 'no vacancy' sign for the motel rooms was often lit up. The lounge and bar were popular with the young men and women. A trusted worker, my responsibilities varied depending on the needs: switchboard, coat check, room service, bus boy, banquet waiter and 'gofer'. Too young to be working in the bar, I was close enough to see what was happening around it, and into the dance hall; I enjoyed the music of the live bands that played at the discothèque. One of the songs that has remained with me over the years is called 'How Can I be Sure?' The lyrics reflected my state of mind; I was never sure if I was doing the right thing, or trusting the right people. Indeed in a 'world that's constantly changing,' would I find my calling, my place, my passion?

'In a few minutes, we'll see the lights of Dalhousie,' I said.

'Are you talking about people or real lights?' Norman said.

'Both!' I said.

Overlooking the river, on the west side of town is the St. John Bosco cemetery where my grandparents were buried. Their headstone is close to the main gate so even at that late hour of the day, although I couldn't read the words on the monuments, I knew exactly where to look. Would my parents be buried there as well? Would I? So many thoughts crossed my mind in those final moments of our trip back to our hometown. It wasn't the greatest place on earth to be from but that night I didn't want to refer to it as the 'lousy town'. One's birthplace is special despite all its flaws.

Two minutes later, we had arrived at 626 Victoria Street.

28

Have You Any Bengay?

In September 1973, I moved to Moncton to study French-English translation and interpretation. My friend Dave, already enrolled at the Université de Moncton, was instrumental in helping me adjust to this new environment. A room was available where he boarded and Dave helped me get settled which eased the move to unchartered territory. We were across the hall from each other on the second floor of a small house at 140 Jones Street, a thirty minute walk to campus.

Situated in south eastern New Brunswick in the Petitcodiac River Valley, Moncton serves as a distribution hub as it lies at the geographic centre of the Maritime provinces. Moncton was founded by the Pennsylvania Dutch immigrants from Philadelphia in 1766. However, earlier settlers included the French Acadians who established a marshland farming community in 1773 not far from Moncton called Le Coude. Fort Beauséjour was captured by English forces in 1755 under the command of Lt. Col. Robert Monckton. In that same year the Acadians were expelled from all areas of British control but eventually came back to resettle in all three of the Maritime provinces and the Gaspé coast. You often see Acadian flags on the south side of the Gaspé coast.

Thanks to the Canadian National Railways which established locomotive repairs shops in the city and the T. Eaton Company which opened a catalogue mail order business employing more than 700 people, the city grew exponentially. Approximately two thirds of the population today are English speaking while nearly one-third speak French. The largest French-language University in Canada outside Quebec, l'Université de Moncton enrols over 4,000 students a year.

Smaller than Saint John but much larger than Fredericton, the capital city, Moncton appealed to me because of its dual English-French culture.

Through Dave, I met a lot of people, not all of them associated with the university. Some were gay friends that he had met at house parties. It took some time for me to feel comfortable in this new city but eventually I enjoyed all facets of this unique bilingual environment.

Moncton being only three and a half hours away from Dalhousie, I was able to visit my parents regularly. On one of these visits, Dave and I travelled together. Back in Dalhousie, we would each visit our own families. One incident in the fall of 1973 remains vivid in my mind. Dave had come by and was sitting in the kitchen while I was ironing a shirt I wanted to wear that evening; a white seer-suckered shirt which had been bought in Montreal on one of our trips to the big city. My sister was asking about my Christmas plans, wanting to know when I would arrive in Dalhousie and how long I intended to stay. Without looking at her, I said that I was going to the Caribbean for Christmas with my friend Douglas. Sensing that this would not sit well with her, I avoided looking in her direction and it must have been obvious that I was uncomfortable about this discussion. She pursued by asking who would pay for the trip; I answered that Douglas had kindly offered to cover all my expenses. She replied, 'he must be gay!' With my head bent towards the ironing board and looking at Dave from the corner of my eye, I responded by saying, 'Yes dear, and so am I!'

The tension in the room was palpable. Nothing was said for several minutes—which felt like an eternity to me. In my mind, my sister must have known that I was gay so the shock should not have been too great. Would she tell mother? I spoke without thinking of the consequences of my words; I hoped to God that I hadn't burned any bridges. It was a great relief when someone finally came into the room; the change of conversation was like a breath of fresh air. It would be another year before I felt comfortable enough to open up to my sister.

Not alone in my desire to be honest about my sexual orientation, Dave also had his share of tensions with *his* family. In those days, coming out of the closet was risky. One would tread carefully, perhaps sending trial balloons to get a reaction and then decide on an appropriate strategy to broach such a sensitive topic. Our quick weekend visits to Dalhousie were too rushed to prepare the groundwork for making what could amount to a critical announcement. Dave and I agonised on how best to approach this delicate situation. For his part, Norman had had no problems when he told his mother; it was not entirely surprising as she was out and about, and probably knew many gay men. However, he felt he was being shunned by his father although there were no overt displays of rejection.

'You'll never believe what just happened to me,' Dave said. 'I was sitting in my room upstairs when I hear my Mom call me from the ground floor. I heard her say –'How long have you been gay?'

'What?' I replied.

And she repeated her question, saying 'Do you have any Bengay, for arthritis?'

'Flustered, I rushed down the stairs and handed her what she had asked for,' he said. 'She looked at me rather strangely; I was trying hard not to look shocked.'

She had probably figured out the unintended double meaning. *As-tu du Bengay?* sounded like *How long have you been gay?*

'Do you think she understood?' I said.

'I wonder; I really don't know for sure,' he said.

Dave was nearing the end of his years in Moncton and his relationship with Homer. By the following Spring, just after graduation, he moved to Montreal, the city of his dreams where he began employment with the St. Lawrence Seaway Corporation. Gradually, he would fade from the picture; however, I would always visit his parents as they had been so dear to me when I was in high school in Dalhousie.

29

Surprise! I'm Here!

It was past eleven P.M. when Norman dropped me off at my parents' home. Walking up the driveway and into the back yard, I waved to the lady next door. Agnes, known to all in our parish as *ma Tante Pitoune*, admits to three passions: praying, making fudge and playing bingo; an elderly woman, was amazingly agile and alert for her years. Her broad smile was a great welcome to me.

The kitchen door had been left open and I could see my mother sitting at the table looking at recipe books. Hearing noises coming from the yard, she raised her head; she was not sure who she was seeing. As I came into the house, she screamed with joy. My father jumped up from his living room chair and came to greet me. Surprised by my unplanned and unexpected visit, my father decided that this called for a drink. The vodka and the rum were brought out and drinks were served.

The details of their upcoming Globus tour to Western Europe were revealed over the next few days. Dad was anxious to leave and Mom was somewhat apprehensive, although excited at the thought of going on a long trip with him. My father told me that since June when my mother retired, she had been catching up on rest and sleep. In fact, he seemed a bit worried that she might not have enough energy to make the journey as she spent almost every afternoon napping on the living room sofa. I told my father that she would certainly perk up once they set foot in London on the first day of the bus tour.

Privately, my father mentioned how he had meticulously planned this trip so that my mother would be leaving town just days before schools were scheduled to reopen for the fall semester. My mother's passion for teaching was obvious to anyone who knew her; being away at that critical time of the year made sense. Not fond of extreme heat, both my parents had always favoured holidays in the spring or the fall. September in Europe would be the perfect antidote for a retiring teacher.

I appreciated not having to answer the eternal question of 'when do you plan to marry?' or 'have you met the right girl?'

Since my Mother knew I was gay, it was a settled matter; I wasn't coming home with a girl nor was I planning to get married!

Five years prior, while touring the eastern provinces with Jack, my partner at the time, we had stopped in Dalhousie to spend the night. Jack was older than I, and my mother had immediately noticed the age difference between us. Her non-verbal expressions showed that she was uncomfortable with the situation; however, she said nothing to me about it. Jack had made a strong impression on her and before we left Dalhousie, I could sense that the wall of apprehension was coming down.

30

A Christmas in Florida

Christmas in the Steeves family had never strayed from the usual; customs and traditions were followed, festive treats were repeated from year to year and everyone gathered in the house in which we grew up. It was usually very cold at Christmas time but that did not seem to matter to anyone or so I thought. I can't recall who suggested that we should spend the holidays in Florida, but I certainly remember that I was not in favour of it. Although I had been eager to go on a Caribbean vacation a year earlier, I couldn't see myself spending Christmas and New

Year's with my family in the south. As I didn't want to offend my parents, I agreed to go along and make the best of it.

Arrangements were made for a rental unit in Indian Rocks, just north of St. Petersburg, Florida. We flew into Tampa on December 22nd 1975, and were met by Patsy, my sister Claire's friend. She had met Patsy at a workshop organised by her employer, the Government of New Brunswick. They had immediately struck up a friendship that had gone on long after their meeting in Bathurst.

Patsy, who lived in upstate New York, regularly spent time with her parents who had a winter home in Tampa. As she was visiting her family in Florida for the holidays, she and Claire would be able to spend time together. Had Patsy suggested to Claire a family Christmas holiday in the sun?

On our second day in Indian Rocks, Patsy came over for a visit. Mother asked her to stay for dinner which she graciously accepted. Meal preparation reminded me of the days when we did family summer trips in which my mother had everything packed in coolers and boxes ready to serve a hungry family.

I was intrigued by Patsy for several reasons: she drove an old Mercedes-Benz and was much older than Claire. It appeared that she came from a family of means which was certainly not our situation. She was highly educated with a Ph.D. in psychology. Refined and classy, I admired her ability to communicate flawlessly.

Later in the evening when the dinner dishes had been washed and put away, Patsy and Claire decided to go for a drive around town; they asked me to join them. We couldn't have asked for a better tour guide, Patsy knew her way around and was able to provide interesting commentary on all of the places that we drove by. At one point, she suggested that we should go 'to my cousin's place'. My immediate reaction, which I kept to myself, was 'Why on earth would I come this far to visit someone's relative that I never met?' I kept silent in the hope that the idea would fade or that something better would surface. Why protest? It would appear unappreciative and would only make matters worse, I thought to myself.

We drove for another twenty minutes before Patsy parked and shut the motor.

'Well, we're here,' she said. 'Let's go in.'

'This is a bar,' I said. 'I thought we were visiting a relative, Patsy.'

'Let's have a drink, shall we?' she said. 'We don't have to stay if you don't want to.'

Just above the main door was a huge sign: 'My Cousin's Place'. There was no indication of the type of establishment we were entering but it was plainly obvious once we were inside. This was a gay bar. At first, I thought the choice had been made because Claire knew I was gay. But what happened next floored me. Claire looked at Patsy, then turned to me and said 'I wasn't sure how to tell you.'

I had had my doubts about my sister but I think I preferred not to dwell on it. I wasn't about to ask her about her sexual orientation; she would have to tell *me*. Now it felt great to have an ally; our conversations could be far more open and frank.

The exhilaration I felt that evening was indescribable. I was happy that she had found it in her heart to come out to me—which meant she trusted me. Riding high in the back seat of the Mercedes, we headed back for Indian Rocks where we spent the rest of the week.

We managed to attend midnight mass in a Catholic church but everywhere, everything seemed odd. It was like having Christmas in the middle of July. Santa without snow made no more sense than igloos in the desert. Every once in a while, I reminded myself of the date; hearing Jingle Bells outside a shopping centre where people were wearing shorts made some sense but was incongruous because of the heat.

At the end of our vacation, we concluded that it had been enjoyable despite the fact that it was surreal most of the time. None of us was sure that we would do it again, but we were glad we had experienced it at least once. I went back to Moncton for my final semester feeling good about the holiday and happy that my sister Claire and I would be able to be a lot more open with each other.

A few months later, it was time again to visit my parents. Little did I know that the moment of truth would be upon me by coming home for a weekend! My parents didn't have a rule about regular visits to Dalhousie but they were nonetheless expected and appreciated.

The kitchen was the focus in our home, where discussions were held and decisions taken. It was also where we gathered in the evenings to socialize. During a weekend stay in the spring of 1975, my mother and I sat up at the kitchen table talking about family issues. Conversations flowed much easier if she had had a drink or two; however, she never went beyond what was, in her mind, a reasonable amount of liquor.

That night, she poured herself one stiff drink and shared her concerns with me. I suspect that she did the same with other visiting siblings. Anyone who had lived in a small community knows how gossip can ruin people's lives. My mother was not about to tell anyone her innermost feelings, not even her best friends for fear that her words would be repeated. She was a very private person; only the immediate family members were allowed in the inner sanctum.

Neither was she the type to ambush anyone, let alone her own flesh and blood. That same evening, she rambled on about one of my brother's woes but I could feel that she would eventually come around to talk about something that concerned *me*. Sensing her discomfort, I felt unsure what to say to make her more relaxed. A break in the dialogue made matters worse; I was getting nervous without knowing why.

Suddenly, out of the blue, she told me that her sister, Aunt Annie, told her that Mike, her own son, and I were 'sissies'. I was lost for words. Nothing came out of my mouth. Should I refute this? Why should I deny what she obviously knew, what she had probably sensed for years but had remained silent? The tears rolled down her face as I held back mine.

After getting her composure back, she went into a diatribe blaming herself for my sexual orientation. No amount of consolation would help; she was hurt and nothing I could say was going to heal the wound. I excused myself and went upstairs to bed not knowing how she would react the next morning nor how things would work out in the long run.

It had been my greatest mistake, the thing I regret the most in my life. I should have been upfront and told her instead of being afraid and let her find out from someone else. I knew *she* knew; all mothers know when they have a gay son. I could have explained it to her in a more humane way. I could have told her about my feelings; I could have explained that it had nothing to do with my upbringing and that she needn't cry over it. It was a sad error on my part, one that would haunt me for the rest of my life.

Although I felt relieved that things were now in the open, it took both my mother and I a bit time before we were comfortable being around each other. The love between us pulled us through and we never again talked about my homosexuality. She may never have understood that it wasn't a choice I was making but rather an acceptance of what I couldn't change.

By sharing her grief about her own son, had Aunt Annie found any solace in telling my mother that they each had a gay offspring? Professionally, she had done well with her life; perhaps she felt that she had not been the mother she should have been and that this was her punishment. Had there been a Parents and Friends of Lesbians and Gays (PFLAG) chapter in town, Aunt Annie would have been its president. She believed that being gay was not a choice, that it was genetic and that no amount of brainwashing would change a person's sexual orientation.

I had never imagined being *pulled* 'out of the closet' by my own mother. For years, I had thought of ways of telling her but finding just the right time and manner to confirm her suspicions followed me like an albatross. All of that anxiety had been dissipated in a matter of minutes but not in a way that I had wanted. It had been foolish of me to think that I could procrastinate on such an important revelation central to my being. She had trumped me with her best and highest card in her hand as she had done so many times playing bridge.

In the years that followed, we never went back to the topic of sexual orientation; perhaps because she did not understand it or that she felt it was taboo, I would never know. Despite having had the rug pulled out from under me, I was happy about one thing: she would know about the real me before passing away.

31

Labour Day Weekend

The Labour Day weekend visit to Dalhousie was over in a flash. My parents wondered why I had bothered to travel one thousand kilometres for such a short stay. They were pleased that I had come before their overseas trip. Together we talked about the people they would meet on the tour and how Mom would likely make new friends. After all, she was gregarious and loved meeting people.

Dad had travelled extensively during the war when he was young, but this transatlantic flight would be a first for both of them. My mother had been frightened during a lightening storm while flying from Halifax to Barbados. Had this incident made her afraid of flying? It was best not to mention it so as to not create any unnecessary anxieties.

In the wee hours of Monday morning, Norman and I began the long trek back to Ottawa. The return trip seemed shorter and less gruelling partly because we gained an hour crossing into the province of Quebec. We drove for a few hours before sunrise.

'So how was the weekend?' Norman said.

'It went by way too fast,' I said.

'Everything OK in the Steeves household?' he said.

'Nothing out of the ordinary to report,' I said.

'Are you happy that you visited your parents before their trip abroad?' Norman said.

'Oh yes!' I said. 'My parents were so happy to see me. For the first time in a long while, my mother looked relaxed. We stayed up and had our usual drinks in the kitchen every night. There were no family issues to talk about, no big decisions to make and no looming problems to fret about. The talk was all about the upcoming holiday. My father did mention that he felt my Mom was sleeping far more than usual which made him worry about her stamina for the three weeks they would be touring.'

'Are you worried about that?' Norman said.

'I think my father is forgetting that when he retired two years ago, he too had been extremely tired and slept a lot,' I said. 'Sitting in his easy chair in the living room, he would nod off and have forty winks several times a day. I don't think he understands the level of fatigue Mom has is in part due to the years of teaching, plus dealing with her arthritis. Not surprising that she needs to rest up to gather her strength for what will be an exhausting hop around Europe. They are visiting seven countries in 21 days never spending more than one night in each location. Just thinking about it makes me tired.'

'I sure hope they have a good trip,' Norman said. 'Your mother waited a long while for this opportunity.'

The rolling hills around Cabano seemed to move in sync with the waltz of the clouds. The clumps of trees on the green knolls stood perfectly as though they had been arranged by a horticulturist. These uplifting panoramas reminded me of scenes in some of the Italian renaissance art on display at the National Art Gallery in Ottawa. Would Mom and Dad see similar scenes on their way from Geneva to Rome? It made me happy to think that my mother who, years ago, had tried so hard to show us the beauty in our own country was now herself going to be exposed to foreign destinations that would open her eyes to new stimuli.

We were almost at the end of highway 185 which is near the city of Rivière-du-Loup. As we got closer, we could see the St. Lawrence Seaway. The sight of that mighty body of water reminded me of the first time I saw it on a family trip with my parents. On seeing the seaway, my mother had started to sing '*C'est sur le bord du St. Laurent...*' a well-known French Canadian folk song.

32

Living Vicariously

Nearing our destination, we talked about upcoming events in the Capital.

'Do you remember hearing the owner of that store sing ABBA's 'Dancing Queen' at seven o'clock on a Saturday morning?' I said.

Norman didn't need to respond to that question. We both knew how funny it had been to hear her sing at the top of her lungs all the wonderful ABBA songs that came out in the late 1970's. How could we be angry with her? We loved those songs; we sang along with her enjoying the upbeat mood carried by those tunes.

'Going to the Chez Henri tomorrow night?' I said.

'That's an idea,' Noman said. 'If you're not too tired, you could come too.'

'I really prefer going to Sacs,' I said. 'However, I could have a beer with you and Marc then move on to Sacs for the disco music.'

Back in Ottawa in record time and before dark, Norman dropped me off on O'Connor Street. I unlocked the door to my apartment, put on some music and spent the next few hours playing back in my mind all the events of the weekend. Thankful that all had gone well and that I was back in time to go to work the next day, I meditated on my good fortune in life: my parents, my siblings, my health, my job, my friends and my home.

Just as I got back in the nation's capital, the Progressive Conservative Party of Canada, led by Brian Mulroney, won 211 seats in the House of Commons, forming the largest majority government in Canadian history. The world was changing; nothing stayed the same. Still, I had my family that I could count on which brought a great measure of stability to my life. I recalled the lyrics to 'How Can I be Sure?' and even though I was sure about nothing, I felt a lot more confident and content about my life.

In bed, before falling asleep, I was already anticipating the postcards from Europe. They would be well chosen to show what they had seen. It would be written by my mother in her usual tidy script and addressed by my father in square block letters aligned perfectly. Europe had been on my travel plans but I did not have the disposable income to allow me that luxury. I would live vicariously through the missives sent by my parents.

33

Postcards from Europe

In early October, I received a postcard from my parents which had been mailed from somewhere in Holland. As I had expected, my mailing address had been written by my father and the notes by my mother. Instead of the usual perfect script, her handwriting was barely legible. Must have been written when the bus was moving, I thought to myself. By the time the card arrived in Ottawa, my parents were on their way back to Canada.

A similar postcard had been received by my sister. No sooner had they arrived back in Dalhousie, she called them to find out about the trip. My Dad did most of the talking before passing the phone over to my Mom. She sounded rather lethargic according to Claire. Her condition was attributed to jet lag which my mother had really never experienced before. A few days later, another call was made, and still my mother did not sound any better. She said that she was fine and would likely be *up and at 'em* in a matter of days.

Claire had a suspicion that all wasn't well so she decided to make the trip from Halifax to Dalhousie; she would make her own assessment of our mother's condition. When she arrived, my mother was sitting in my father's easy chair in the living room looking old and frail and not at all the proud person she had always been. *No*, she hadn't been to see a doctor and *yes* that might be a good idea. An appointment was made with a local doctor who ordered a series of tests. Even before the results were available, the attending physician suggested that she be brought to Moncton for a computerised tomography (CT) scan.

Arrangements were made for her hospitalisation at the Moncton General and for my father to board with friends who lived not too far from the medical campus. They motored to Moncton with mother still not showing any signs of improvement. The three and a half hour journey was not easy for her. The admitting procedures went quickly as the hospital in Dalhousie had sent some of the supporting documentation ahead of time; a semi-private room was made available for her. Once settled in her room, my father and Claire drove to the Godin's house on Everett Street. That evening, he ate very little and hardly said a word.

Tests were scheduled over the next few days. We all waited anxiously for the results. My mother had always been strong and healthy. Despite the pain of arthritis, she had managed to do what she wanted. Whatever was happening to her body, she did not understand; it did not make sense to her. If she had any fears, she did not share them with anyone. Stoic and full of resolve, she would fight this as much as she could. She had fought against arthritis all her life and it hadn't gotten the best of her. She would certainly be up for this new fight, whatever it was.

The news was devastating; an inoperable brain tumour. Could this be a mistake? Had they done all the right tests? We had no reason to doubt the competent people at the Moncton General but the look on Father's face was enough for them to suggest that it would probably be a good idea for us to get a second opinion, not that they had any reason to believe that she had been misdiagnosed but rather to help us come to accept the inevitable.

Staff at the Moncton General suggested that my mother be brought to the Victoria General in Halifax; they would have an ambulance take her there.

34

Countering Negative Thoughts

How anyone copes in difficult times is a mystery; yet most people find ways to go about their daily chores all the while dealing with painful issues. October in Ottawa is a busy social time of the year for me with house parties, outings, plays and concerts at the National Arts Centre.

Public Broadcasting Services in the United States was airing 'The Brain Series' on Wednesday evenings. Had it not been for my mother's condition, I'm not sure this series would have been of interest to me; however, in the current state of affairs, I was really keen on finding out as much as I could about the brain and how it functions. The show was very good, well documented and in plain English; listeners were informed of the complexity of this misunderstood part of the anatomy.

When a door closes, somewhere a window opens as they expression goes. I remembered this fondly from a scene in the musical The Sound of Music. My mother's illness and her decline were like having a door close very slowly. I tried to keep myself busy and not dwell constantly on her condition. When a call came for a local school board asking if I could conduct a ten week Continuing Ed. course on the topic of interior decoration, I jumped at the offer. I prepared a syllabus, mailed it to them and waited for a response. With very little training to my credit, I nevertheless felt capable of delivering a credible course based on notes I had kept from an interior decorating correspondence program I had taken between the time I left Canadian Imperial Bank of Commerce and before I joined Irving Oil.

An aficionado of figure skating, watching the sport live or on television was the perfect escape for me during this period. Towards the end of October of that year, I spent many hours watching the Skate Canada competitions. It was easy to forget what was going on with my family and in the world when I was glued to the television set for hours on end admiring the skill and grace of these young people. I could sense their passion for the sport; the drive and determination for success was inspiring.

For brief periods I was able to escape the realities pressing around me by watching this figure skating or by keeping busy with household chores. I tried to focus on what I was doing as opposed to what I was feeling. If I could suppress, even for short periods of time, the anger and the fear I felt about losing my mother, I was able to gather enough courage and strength to counter the *negative* thoughts that clouded my mind.

35

Mother's Destiny

Having my mother in Halifax at the Victoria General made things a bit easier. My Dad stayed with my sister and together they would visit my mother every day. A battery of tests was done quickly which included a magnetic resonance imaging (MRI) test. The family gathered to meet with the specialists to hear the diagnosis. In a small room at the hospital, we were told of the grim prognosis. Their conclusions were the same as the Moncton medical team. A biopsy would tell us more about the tumour.

The team of oncologists explained that a brain tumour is a mass of abnormal cells which can either be non-cancerous (benign) or cancerous (malignant). Options for treatment depend on type, size and location of the tumour. One of the symptoms is the gradual loss of sensation or movement in an arm or a leg. Clearly that had been the case with my mother; it explained why her handwriting on the postcards had been so unlike her normal perfectly-formed script. From pictures that were taken early on in the trip, she is seen holding her left arm as if it was limp. She apparently admitted to my father that something was happening to her but chalked it up to fatigue. In hindsight, it appeared that the onset of the problem started during the flight from Montreal to London. According to medical literature, weakness caused by a brain tumour can be very similar to weakness caused by a stroke.

In my mother's case, the malignant tumour was lodged in the forehead aligned between her two eyes. There was no possibility of removing it surgically as it was located in an inaccessible area; therefore, the only options were radiation and chemotherapy. We were asked what we thought of the proposed treatments; we all agreed that their suggestions made sense but that the final decision should be left to her.

We left the hospital feeling very sad and powerless. There was nothing we could do to reverse her destiny. Our role would be to support her through an ordeal about which we knew very little.

The shock and grief caused by this diagnosis was felt by all of us in the family. Why her? Without saying much to each other, we knew that she was unlikely to be alive at Christmas.

36

Getting Ready for the Inevitable

The grey days of November were upon us; everything looked bleak. Known in the Catholic Church as the *month of the deceased*, November has always been very sombre for me. Maybe it's my imagination, but there seems to be much fewer days of sunshine during that month; rain and wind are the norm. Trees, having lost their leaves, stand as grey pillars amid the concrete and pavement of our inner cities. The vibrant colours of autumn are replaced with muted tones of brown, grey and black. 'Macabre' comes to mind as a word that best describes my feelings during this, the penultimate month of the year.

As the year comes to an end, so do the lives of many; obituaries seem to double in length when the cold and dreary days of November set in. Would my mother be called back? How could I be expected to go to work every day and still be productive? Colleagues offered their moral support; having lost someone close, some friends guided me in my preparation for the inevitable.

Grief takes many forms; it starts from the time you know that death is inevitable. I was ill-prepared for the stage of grief that occurs prior to death; the feeling of loss and abandonment creeps in without warning. Was I giving up hope by grieving so soon? Only a miracle could have changed the nightmare my mother was facing. Death itself may not hurt but pain and anguish leave indelible marks. It was hell for me to be in Ottawa while my mother was lying near death in Halifax. However difficult it was for me, I was sure it was nothing compared to the agony that my mother faced on a daily basis. She was so enraged; angry with God for letting her down. I think the fear of dying, along with leaving this world so young, caused her more pain and anguish than the tumour and chemo.

It would have been so much easier to see my mother dying slowly of old age; dying in her sleep. That's the way I had hoped my parents would go. I had always imagined that my father would go first as my mother was stronger; she would fend for herself rather well in old age, I would think to myself. Events were unfolding completely contrary to the neat tidy plans I had kept in the back of my mind. As a family, we would need to work together so that my father would not be wanting for anything. That he was unable or untrained to make a meal, was of great concern to us all. But now was not the time to think about such things; this would have to wait; we would cross that bridge when we came to it.

Claire called to say that she was hoping I could come to Halifax as soon as possible. I felt the stress in her voice. It was demanding for her to have us all in her home; however, it did help bring us together, we drew strength from one another. The airplane trip to Halifax was uneventful and I remember very little about it as I was in a daze. As much as I like to travel, there was no pleasure to be had on that trip.

37

Tears in His Soup

As expected, Mom decided on full treatment regardless of side effects or consequences. She was fighting for her life and she would give it her best. Down the hall, was a close friend of hers, Diane, who was on her last days following a brain tumour as well. The names of other women from Dalhousie who had had brain tumours surfaced. Was it the pollution from the paper mill? Was it something in the drinking water? Diane was also a retired school teacher. Could these tumours be related to the stress of the teaching profession? There were no answers forthcoming.

By mid November, Mom had completed her radiation treatment. The chemotherapy was delivered intravenously. Within days, results were apparent. The loss of hair was probably the most obvious, which seemed to bother me more than it bothered her. Her hair was important; she used to go regularly to the hairdresser. She loved having someone play with her hair. When much younger, I had often blow-dried her hair and combed it out. It was therapeutic for her; I could have been at it for hours. It was pure joy; a treat she relished fondly. Now, almost balding, she didn't seem to care about her appearance. In fact, a box of Quality Street chocolates, brought to her by my Dad, was eaten up in record time. Gaining weight and ill-fitting her clothes did not bother her. Did she know her time was up?

At Claire's home we cried, we laughed and we planned as best we could with the limited information we had. Every day, for over a week, we drove to the hospital to be with Mom. Speech became difficult; she was at a loss for words. When trying to find the word for 'toothpick,' the closest she would come was 'clothes pin'. Both made of wood, we understood what she wanted. This made her laugh which lightened up the atmosphere in the room.

My father who had always relied so much on my mother was about to lose his lifetime partner and he knew it. He kept this emotion to himself but once in a while it would come out quite unexpectedly. While having lunch in a restaurant on South Park Street, after a particularly difficult visit with Mom, tears from my father's eyes flowed down from his cheeks into his soup. It was heart-wrenching to witness the sadness of a man who had waited years to retire to have his soul-mate taken away from him so quickly. His reliance on her made us wonder if her eventual passing would bring him down as well.

In her final weeks in Halifax, she questioned her religion; it was as if she had lost all of her faith in her creator. The unfairness of an early death preyed on her mind. Repeatedly, she asked: Why me? Why now? Her inability to communicate clearly made it hard for her to express her pain and anger; it was nonetheless clearly visible on her face. We all felt so powerless in the face of this tragedy.

In an about-face, my mother's faith took centre stage, contrary to her feelings just days before. Calmness returned; she seemed at peace. After being angry with her God, she accepted her fate; lovingly, she looked at us as if she wanted to make sure she wouldn't forget the faces of the people that had meant so much to her. Slowly, she relied more and more on simple phrases and gestures as a way of communicating with us.

My father remained in Halifax with my sister while the rest of the family went back to our respective homes. As the weeks went on, there was little that the doctors could do for her. The chemo and radiation had not been entirely successful; it had been a way of buying time and to have her with us for longer. However, there was little quality of life left for her; she was showing signs of being ready to go.

Palliative care was discussed with the medical authorities at the Halifax General. As there was little that could be done for her at this point, keeping her comfortable and out of pain would be the primary objective. By early December, a decision had been made that she would be transferred to the Dalhousie Hospital.

No longer the facility it had been in its heyday, the Dalhousie Hospital had been turned into a palliative care centre. Opened in 1952, just in time for my birth, I was the first of my siblings to be born in the new hospital. It was operated by the Daughters of Jesus, the same order of nuns who ran most of the Catholic schools in northern New Brunswick. They were able to attract excellent physicians and a few good surgeons; the hospital had an excellent reputation. Years later when the concept of regional health centres took hold, it was decided that a new hospital should be located where there was a large population base.

Campbellton was selected as the ideal location; slowly the hospital in Dalhousie lost its funding and departments closed one after the other. I found it sad; the fabric of my home town was wearing thin.

My mother would pass away in the same building where she gave birth to me. It was a bizarre feeling, one that I tried hard not to dwell on. If only I could take her place; she could live on and I would be the one to pass away. She would probably have thought the same had it been the reverse situation. The only saving grace is that she would not see one of her own go before her. That would have been the worst possible situation for her.

38

Regrouping

An early snow in the Nation's Capital had people feeling festive; the traditional lighting of the trees on Parliament Hill brought hordes of people to Centretown. Shoppers were out in droves; stores were busier than usual. The economy was booming across the country; the markets were strong. Everywhere I looked, I saw positive signs; reassuring as it was, I was not feeling upbeat.

It seemed that most of my friends had their birthdays in December; I was invited to birthday parties and Christmas parties. Not wanting to put a damper on the season's festivities,

I avoided accepting invitations to large groups of people preferring instead the comfort of several close friends.

I made plans to return 'Down East' knowing very well that this would be the final chapter. The ending was undeniable: together, we would face the music as best we could. Humour and the love of friends and relatives would help us get through this.

39

In Death and in Laughter

We gathered at the homestead in Dalhousie to start the final vigil. My mother was now in a coma at the Dalhousie Hospital and wasn't expected to live very long. How long, nobody knew. Weeks away from Christmas, the festive season had no meaning for any of us. No decorations were put up; nobody spoke about Christmas. Visits to the hospital were much more difficult. It was my first experience of being in a room with a comatose person. I could not bring myself to speak to her although I was aware that, even in a comatose state, people can hear.

Huddled together in the family home in which we grew up, it was good to be back under the same roof at the same time even if the reason for the reunion was not a cheery one. Even in dark times, we always found things to laugh about. Even in the saddest of circumstances, there was always something out of the ordinary that got us howling with laughter. My mother's good humour had been passed on in the genes. Every now and then, someone would invoke one of her hilarious or corny sayings which brought her back to be with us, even if temporarily.

On the morning of December 16th, the telephone rang at about 6:30 a.m. There was no doubt about the reason for this call at that hour of the day. Mother had passed away all alone in her hospital room. The night before, several of the nurses had told us that the end was near. There were obvious signs but these had not registered with any of us.

My brother Phil and I decided that we would take care of the funeral arrangements; my parents had pre-arranged their funerals years earlier. Claire would take care of getting clothes ready for us to take to the embalmer. Calls to Mitchell's Funeral Home went unanswered, which was unusual as there was always someone there during business hours. It didn't help anyone's stress level.

'Everybody's dying to get in,' Phil said.

'They must be having cold cuts at a Christmas party somewhere,' I said.

This kind of black humour was most unusual for us; it did nonetheless help relieve the tension that had been mounting since early October.

In my mother's final days, her body swelled considerably to the point that she hardly looked herself. A very proud woman, she would have been horrified to have anyone see her as she was. The decision to have a closed coffin was made without dissent. The casket would be opened for private family viewing just minutes before leaving for the church service. At the appointed time, I chose to leave the room, not wanting to have that image of my mother haunt me for the rest of my days.

The wake lasted three days, as was customary in our neck of the woods. Each afternoon and each evening, visitors came to pay their respects. A huge picture of Mom, placed on the casket, had been taken at her retirement party. Could she not have deserved a few good years in retirement?

A stream of fellow teachers, some retired, some still on active duty, paid their respects. In a matter of a few days, I heard stories about my mother that I found most interesting: she had been well liked and many had looked up to her. Some had confided in her knowing that whatever she had been told would never be repeated. She obviously knew how to keep a secret. She shared her deepest thoughts with us but never did she betray the trust others had placed in her.

Relatives from both sides of the family, still in shock at my mother's early passing, stood by us during the wake. Aunt Céline marvelled at how we were all coping with grief. Having lost her husband in her late 20s, she knew that the grace of God would get us through the difficult moments. I understood what she was saying as I felt a wave of energy and support without knowing where it was coming from. Suspecting that I would feel the pain after it was all over, I allowed myself to enjoy this rush of positive energy.

My father's two sisters provided some comic relief as they came to the funeral parlour in the very same outfit. Unknowingly, they had gone shopping in the same store to find a suitable dress for the occasion. The look of horror on their faces when they realised that they both had bought the same dress at Dalfen's was priceless. I wondered if my mother had anything to do with it.

Friends and neighbours brought food to the house so that we did not need to worry about meal preparation. I hadn't expected that old tradition to be still alive in 1984. There was food for an army; it kept coming in faster than we could consume it.

Ron's mother (Aunt Jennie), who lived next door to us, came over to gather bed linens which needed washing. That simple act of kindness was out of the ordinary. Only a person having been through a death in the family would have known how appreciated that would be.

I don't recall much of the funeral mass as I was on another planet. My sister Claire did the first reading; I could tell she was struggling to keep control. It was admirable of her to want to do so under considerable grief. The church choir did their best as they struggled with music difficult to perform at the best of times.

The ground was frozen; burial would follow in the spring. *Praise the Lord*, I thought; *the traditional procession to the cemetery was not going to happen.* As an altar boy, I had witnessed countless heart-wrenching burials. I was not eager to see my mother's casket lowered into the ground. This was one aspect of the ritual I was happy to avoid.

A few days before Christmas, we took delivery of a flowering plant that had been sent to the house by my mother's sister Irenka. She had wisely stayed at home and not come to the funeral; she would have been very emotional. The potted plant was the *defacto* Christmas tree; it sat on a table next to my mother's favourite chair. It was the only bright spot in an otherwise depressing environment.

40

The Universe Unfolding as it Should

Christmas that year and each one since has never been the same. Was it fair for her to have to leave us so soon? Perhaps she wanted to be the first to go so that she could be spared the eventual loss of her spouse, let alone one of her children preceding her. She had said so repeatedly. It was not as if she had many interests or plans for her retirement years. She had done her fair share of raising kids and taking care of our house. It was time for a good rest. But did she really wish for 'eternal' rest'?

Phil and Clare talked about how they would ensure proper care for our father, who was 65 now. The focus was moving into a new direction: less talk about my mother, more talk about my father. Once we had settled a number of outstanding issues regarding my father's day-to-day needs, each of us made plans to go back to where we lived. A chapter in my life was coming to a close. For the first time, there was no excitement about the future. It was as if the gold has been rubbed off of the face of the earth. Nothing glittered, nothing appealed to me. I had been told about the time it takes to get over the passing of a parent. Would I be able to let go of the past and embrace the future? Had she given me the skills I needed to transition into a new life?

Over the years that followed, the word 'orphan' crossed my mind often. My mother's sister was most saddened that we had become 'orphaned' and made a big thing of if at the funeral home. This annoying adjective haunted me. I was orphaned by my mother's passing. *Orphelin de la mère* as we say in French. It was as if I felt less than whole because I was Motherless. Yet my mother lives on in me and I do not feel Motherless anymore. I refuse to believe I'm an orphan, as my mother's spiritual presence is always around me. When I need help, I call her. When I want her to intercede on my behalf to be sure to have a safe trip to a foreign land, I simply ask her.

On one of the kitchen walls, just behind the table and chairs, hung a huge poster showing the Fall harvest upon which was printed a poem that my mother read to us when she felt that her words were insufficient to carry the strong message she wished to deliver. Solace would come from the final paragraph of Max Ehrmann' Desiderata:

And whether or not it is clear to you,
no doubt the universe is unfolding as it should.
Therefore be at peace with God,
whatever you conceive Him to be,
and whatever your labors and aspirations,
in the noisy confusion of life keep peace with your soul.
With all its shams, drudgery,
and broken dreams,
it is still a beautiful world.
Be cheerful.

No doubt that the world was unfolding as it should; I just needed to accept that life would go on and take many more unexpected turns and that I was now on my own. Although my world was in disarray, my life had not come to an end.

www.ingramcontent.com/pod-product-compliance
Lightning Source LLC
Chambersburg PA
CBHW030326080526
44584CB00012B/725